# unshaken

## REAL FAITH IN OUR FAITHFUL GOD

### CRAWFORD W. LORITTS JR.

WHEATON, ILLINOIS

*Unshaken: Real Faith in Our Faithful God*

Copyright © 2015 by Crawford W. Loritts Jr.

Published by Crossway
   1300 Crescent Street
   Wheaton, Illinois 60187

Cover design: Jeff Miller, Faceout Studio

Cover image: Shutterstock.com

First printing 2015

Printed in the United States of America

"Take My Hand, Precious Lord." Words and music by Thomas A. Dorsey © 1938 (Renewed) Warner-Tamerlane Publishing Corp. All rights reserved. Used with permission.

All Scripture quotations are from the ESV® Bible (The Holy Bible, English Standard Version®), copyright © 2001 by Crossway, a publishing ministry of Good News Publishers. Used by permission. All rights reserved.

All emphases in Scripture quotations have been added by the author.

Trade paperback ISBN: 978-1-4335-4504-7
ePub ISBN: 978-1-4335-4507-8
PDF ISBN: 978-1-4335-4505-4
Mobipocket ISBN: 978-1-4335-4506-1

---

**Library of Congress Cataloging-in-Publication Data**
Loritts, Crawford W.
 Unshaken : real faith in our faithful God / Crawford Loritts.
  pages cm
 Includes bibliographical references and index.
 ISBN 978-1-4335-4504-7 (tp)
 1. Faith. I. Title.
BV4637.L65 2015
234'.23—dc23           2015001446

---

Crossway is a publishing ministry of Good News Publishers.

| VP | | 25 | 24 | 23 | 22 | 21 | 20 | 19 | 18 | 17 | 16 | 15 |
|----|----|----|----|----|----|----|----|----|----|----|----|----|
| 15 | 14 | 13 | 12 | 11 | 10 | 9 | 8 | 7 | 6 | 5 | 4 | 3 | 2 | 1 |

To

Fellowship Bible Church

I am so grateful to God for tying our hearts together
and for the great joy and privilege it is to serve you.

# Contents

# Preface

Without faith, there is no Christianity and no Christian living. Faith places the glory, power, and presence of God on display for the world to see and his followers to experience. Faith makes God's people noble, divinely regal, and, at the same time, compellingly attractive. While others "crash and burn," faithful pilgrims keep moving.

These pilgrims are resilient because they know they belong to another world. No matter what happens, they are driven by the pleasure of God and captured by the power and presence of "the Ancient of Days" (Dan. 7:9). Through God's strength and power, they refuse to be defined by circumstances or what happens to them, but, to the contrary, their faith redeems and redefines their circumstances.

And so it should be for us.

But what should be is not always our reality. There is not a follower of Christ who does not at times struggle to reconcile what he knows about God and the seemingly insurmountable challenges and uncertainties he faces. We become fearful, discouraged, and at times frustrated because our faith, frankly, lets us down.

That's why I've written this book. It is my prayer that as you walk through the pages of this book, our great God will pour encouragement into your heart and strengthen your resolve to both believe and act on what he says.

The content of this book is largely framed by a series of messages I preached several years ago at Fellowship Bible Church, where I serve as the senior pastor. My heart was humbled, moved, and deeply encouraged by the response of the people and the apparent way in which the Holy Spirit used the messages to strengthen the faith of many in our congregation. So I share these things with you.

Although I gave those messages several years ago, the Lord made sure that what I am sharing with you in this book is real and fresh in my life. I have written a number of books through the years, but I have never experienced more distractions, challenges, and crises in a given period of time than I did while writing this book. Often the very emphasis or truth I was writing about was exactly what I needed to hear and apply. The book itself was a call for me to exercise faith.

Before we get started, I want to point out that I have not tried to define faith. There's a good reason for this: the Bible does not define faith. However, it describes faith, and I believe that its descriptions of faith will resonate with our hearts and provide clarity. It is difficult for me to define my love for my wife, Karen, but I can describe it in such a way that its meaning is unmistakably clear. So it is with faith.

Please keep these two foundational perspectives in mind as you read these pages:

- First, our journey in this life is about what God wants to do through our lives, not about our using God to accomplish our dreams.
- Second, our impact and effectiveness as followers of Christ is in direct proportion to our faith-filled obedience as we face the challenges and opportunities God places before us.

May our great God fill your heart and mind with such a glorious vision of his power and love that you will see him as greater than all of your fears and more than sufficient to meet all of your needs.

Every book I have written has been a team effort, and *Unshaken* is no exception.

First, I am grateful to God for those who encouraged me to put what was on my heart on paper. God used what I shared in sermon form to bless and encourage many people in our church, as well as those who listen to my messages via podcast and the Internet. The response stirred in me a desire to put those sermons in book form.

This is my first book project with Crossway Books. It is a joy and privilege to work with the Crossway team. Thank you, Lane Dennis, for your leadership and the mission and ministry of Crossway. Thank you, Dave DeWit, for your help and encouragement each step of the way. You are a dear friend and key to making a possibility a reality. Thank you, Greg Bailey, for your thoughtful and helpful insights and your keen editor's eye. I am grateful for the sales and marketing team at Crossway (Amy Kruis, Angie Cheatham, Matt Tully, Janni Firestone, Anthony Gosling, and Ben Thocher). I so appreciate your desire to serve the message of this book by placing it in the hands of as many people as possible.

Thank you, Brandon O'Brien, for your creativity, insights, and helpful suggestions in preparing the manuscript.

Tawnda Holley is my executive assistant. Thank you, Tawnda, for giving order to the constant flow of responsibilities and opportunities that need attention. You helped me to carve out the time to give myself to this very important project.

And then there is Karen. Always Karen. She is the love and

joy of my life. We have been on this faith journey together now for more than forty-four years. Her love and support fills my heart and keeps me pressing forward. She is my bride, my partner in ministry, and my best friend. Thank you, Sweetheart, for encouraging me to be all that God has called me to be and to finish what he has placed in our hands to do.

To God be the glory!

Dr. Crawford W. Loritts Jr.
Atlanta, Georgia
Ephesians 3:20–21

# 1

# God Confidence

Mark Twain once quipped, "All you need in life is ignorance and confidence, and success is sure."[1] There is a bit of truth in that statement. When you either don't care about failing or don't know that you can fail, you typically put your head down and keep plowing ahead.

Do you remember Melanie Oudin? In 2009, the teenage sensation from Marietta, Georgia, took England's Wimbledon tennis tournament by storm. Virtually everyone in the tennis world thought it was a bit of a fluke when she made it past the first round. Everyone, that is, except Melanie. She played like she didn't know that she could lose, exuding an engaging confidence that said, "I belong here with the elite tennis players." There was a passion and sweetness about her that won over the crowd, as well as the announcers. No, she didn't win the tournament. But she did what many thought improbable, if not impossible—she made it through the third round!

That's confidence.

Confidence is the engine that drives achievement. It pushes us toward the mark, the goal. It is the "it factor" that distinguishes the exceptional from the average. Confidence pushes us toward focus and causes us to live with assurance and certainty. According to Merriam-Webster, confidence is "full trust; belief in the power, trustworthiness, or reliability of a person or thing."

But where does it come from?

While it is true that some people seem to have been born with personalities and dispositions that exude a focused self-assurance, for most of us, our confidence has developed over time. Abilities have been sharpened and honed. We have been tested and challenged, and have learned to trust our abilities and capabilities in certain areas. In fact, the challenges have strengthened and refined both our abilities and our will to push forward. The result is a courageous confidence that says, "I don't have to be afraid; this can be done."

The professional athlete doesn't sweat under pressure because he's sunk that shot, hit that ball, and made that catch thousands of times. Chances are the Academy Award–winning actress nurtured and developed her craft for years in relative obscurity and developed an outlook that says, "This may be a bigger stage, but I've been here before and I can do this." The surgeon is focused and calm under pressure because his education, training, and experience have prepared him for that moment. In short, confidence says: "I've been preparing for this very moment. I'm ready. Let's do it."

## CONFIDENCE FROM ABOVE

As followers of Christ, there is a distinctively different basis, direction, and source of our confidence. The Bible speaks of confidence from a vertical perspective. It is not derived from the relative consistency of our experiences and the development of our gifts, talents, and abilities. It doesn't come from the strength of our personalities or our track records of success. Likewise, it is not diminished or damaged by inconsistency, failure, suffering, dysfunction, or what so often appears to be the erratic, unpredictable nature of life.

No. Our confidence is anchored in God. He never changes. He is never out of control. He is never taken by surprise. He never loses. Our circumstances don't affect God; he affects our circumstances. God never missteps. He has no glitches. His ability to function is never overloaded. He never breaks down or crashes. He is our proactive, loving heavenly Father, who not only has a plan for our lives, but also has the resources to make happen everything he intends.

Our confidence does not depend on what we have or what we have done. Our confidence is in a person—our unfailing God, who shows up in every situation, circumstance, and condition in which we find ourselves. This causes us to be resilient, to persevere, to endure.

This kind of confidence is what the Bible calls faith. *Biblical confidence is an enduring faith.*

There's a relationship between the condition and strength of our faith and our view of God. In other words, the condition of our faith is a reflection of our view of God.

But our view of God is often eclipsed by what appear to be insurmountable challenges and difficulties. Added to this is the corrosive cynicism that permeates Western culture. It has become an art form. We have made it intellectually appealing to be doubters. We celebrate our "incisive" negative analysis of seemingly everything and everyone, from the president of the United States to local pastors, from pop icons to our neighbors. Bloggers, magazines, and the tidal wave of talk shows give us a daily autopsy, pointing out what's wrong and why we can't trust this person or that situation. And it affects us. A constant diet of the downside of life lowers our sights, clouds our perspective, and contaminates our faith.

Our faith needs to be guarded and protected, because it is the currency of the Christian life. The writer of the book of Hebrews says it clearly and directly: "And without faith it is impossible to please him, for whoever would draw near to God must believe that he exists and that he rewards those who seek him" (11:6). Our God confidence is no casual thing. It is key to experiencing God's presence and power in our lives and in the circumstances and challenges we face.

Our journey through this life must be viewed through the lens of God's Word. There we see the truth concerning who God is and how we are to face every issue and challenge in life, including those dark, uncertain times. God is there, and he is our confidence.

## ABRAHAM'S GOD-SUSTAINED FAITH

The patriarch Abraham presents a compelling example of a God-sustained confidence—faith—during a dark, seemingly impossible time in his life. He kept believing.

Look closely at the apostle Paul's description of Abraham's enduring faith in Romans 4:16–21:

> That is why it depends on faith, in order that the promise may rest on grace and be guaranteed to all his offspring—not only to the adherent of the law but also to the one who shares the faith of Abraham, who is the father of us all, as it is written, "I have made you the father of many nations"—in the presence of the God in whom he believed, who gives life to the dead and calls into existence the things that do not exist. In hope he believed against hope, that he should become the father of many nations, as he had been told, "So

shall your offspring be." He did not weaken in faith when he considered his own body, which was as good as dead (since he was about a hundred years old), or when he considered the barrenness of Sarah's womb. No unbelief made him waver concerning the promise of God, but he grew strong in his faith as he gave glory to God, fully convinced that God was able to do what he had promised.[2]

I believe four words summarize Paul's description of Abraham's faith. I believe these words represent the core characteristics of enduring faith. Frankly, this is powerful, liberating stuff. It is my prayer that as you embrace these characteristics and their meaning, hope will burst forth in the midst of your trials and opposition.

## Based

The first of the four words is *based*. Abraham's faith was based on something. Verse 21 says that what kept Abraham believing was his conviction "that God was able to do what he had promised." Abraham's confidence was in God's integrity, God's unfailing consistency in doing what he says. God had made a promise to Abraham, and Abraham knew that God always keeps his promises. Notice that *God* had made the promise. Abraham's faith was based on what God had said.

Too many of us have grown discouraged because we have concluded that this faith thing doesn't work. We say: "I desperately wanted God to do something for me. I believed that he would do it. I was full of hope and optimism. But God let me down." The question is, what did we base our faith on? Was it anchored in God's Word? Did he promise to do what we wanted?

Genuine faith and optimism are not the same thing. Granted,

they sometimes appear to be identical since both build our confidence and hope, but that's as far as the similarity goes. Faith is not naive optimism. Optimism can be the wrong kind of faith. At times, it is a foolish confidence that is solely based on desire and not on the promises of God in his Word. As author Paul Miller puts it, optimism can be "childlike trust without the loving father."[3]

Faith does not come up with things for God to do. Faith responds to what God wants done. Faith releases the plans and purposes of God through our lives. Further, there is a relationship between the clear statements and promises in the Word of God and what he places before us or on our hearts to do, become, or accomplish. This is one of the most important anchor lessons in the Christian life.

Some years ago, a man shared with me that his wife had come to believe that if she had enough faith, God was required to do anything she wanted. They had problems in their marriage and were struggling financially. (Hmm, I guess she didn't want God to fix the marriage problems and their finances.) She felt that she and their small child needed to visit relatives in another city. When he told her that they didn't have the money for the trip, she told him—I kid you not—that she and the child were going to the airport, and, by faith, tickets would be waiting for them there. She packed their bags and her husband dropped them off at the airport. Once there, she kept claiming their tickets "by faith," but each time she checked with the ticket agent, there were no tickets. Hours later, she called her husband and asked him to come and take them back home. He did.

Are we sure that our faith is supported by the truth of God's Word? Abraham pressed on because he knew for sure that what he was looking for had been promised by God. He could point back to the clear statements and assurances of God. Let's check the basis of our faith. God honors our faith because he honors his Word. Remember, we're not standing on conjecture or our assumptions. Authentic, life-transforming faith says that we are standing on the promises of God.

## Defies

The second word is *defies*. Enduring faith defies circumstances.

Look again at verses 18 and 19: "*In hope he believed against hope.* . . . He did not weaken in faith when he *considered* his own body, *which was as good as dead* (since he was about a hundred years old), or when he considered the barrenness of Sarah's womb." This is extraordinary.

A key word here is *considered*. Faith is not denial. Abraham stared at his condition, his reality, and said, in essence, "I'm going to believe God anyway." Think about it: God had promised Abraham and Sarah that they would conceive a child through natural means. Abraham was fully aware that he was one hundred years old and that Sarah was ninety. The plumbing didn't work anymore (his body "was as good as dead").

Abraham knew better than to repackage what God had said and try to make the promise happen on his own terms. Remember, he and Sarah had tried that and caused a bit of a mess (Genesis 16). That's a very important lesson for all of us. We shouldn't change what God has said to fit our circumstances. We shouldn't try to make faith "reasonable." The fear of being considered foolish and naive will make us rational but superficial and powerless Christians. Our legacy will be a dead orthodoxy that knows nothing of the supernatural intervention of God and his power to smash through our "realities." We need the impossible and insurmountable so that our concept of God will not be theoretical.

Notice, Abraham squarely faced the reality that there was no way that he and Sarah were going to have a baby on their own. God was going to have to do it.

To refuse to allow the difficulties we face to squelch and temper our faith does not mean that we are living in denial. To be sure, there are those who refuse to accept the harsh reality of their condition or the full weight of their circumstances. Faith does not deny that you have cancer. Faith does not deny that you've lost your job and you're upside down financially. Faith does not deny that your marriage is in a very bad place. Faith does not deny that your children have walked away from the faith. You name it, and faith does not deny its existence. It looks at it. It "considers" it. It examines it. It stares it in the eye, but it says: "*You* don't stop or determine what God wants done. So I stare through you and see my great God, who is able to do what he has promised."

And that's the point. God is most glorified when we are most dependent. All other options are off the table, and the choice is to either throw our hands up in despair or trust all that we have—God. And he's more than enough. He proves himself again and again so that we develop that delightful, defiant resolve that says nothing stops our God.

In a sense, what God called Abraham to believe him for was absurd. But faith is linked to absurdity. If we view faith through the lens of the world, we will be "reasonable" people pleasers, held hostage to conventional wisdom. But in the words of the apostle Paul, "God chose what is low and despised in the world, even things that are not, to bring to nothing things that are, so that no human being might boast in the presence of God"

(1 Cor. 1:28–29). If we are afraid of looking foolish, we will see little if anything of the power and provision of God. Abraham was being set up by God for a miracle.

### Anchored

That leads us to the third word: *anchored.* Enduring faith is anchored in God's omnipotence.

The word *omnipotence* comes from two Latin words that mean "all" (*omni*) and "powerful" (*potent*). God does not just have power; he is the source of all power.

In Romans 4:17, Paul describes the object of Abraham's faith: he is the God "who gives life to the dead and calls into existence the things that do not exist."

A friend of mine owns a successful auto-repair shop. He has very loyal customers because he guarantees his work. If he fails to fix a car to a customer's satisfaction, he makes it right at his expense. In the same way, God stands behind every promise he makes. But unlike my friend, God does not have to correct his work.

We must remember that when God gives us his promise, he is on the line, not we. You see, with God's promises comes his presence. He leads us into impossible, dead situations so that we will experience his power and presence. Every fulfilled promise and deliverance is a declaration of God's glory. So when we choose to turn to God in faith and refuse to allow fear and doubt to cause us to cave in, it's as if God says, "Stand back and watch this." The result is awe and wonder.

Abraham and Sarah's dilemma was designed by God. God did not want them to have a hand in this miracle. He designed their crisis so that his power would be revealed and they could experience it. In fact, this story of God's supernatural intervention was both an anchor and a building block upon which the future of God's people in this world would be built. That's the reason why Paul includes this account as a powerful example of life-altering God confidence.

Abraham represents every follower of Christ. Once we have trusted Christ as our Savior and Lord, we no longer belong to ourselves. We are now his biography. God is writing his story in and through us as we journey through this life. At every turn, he is making a statement concerning his ability, sufficiency, and power to deliver us and lead us through anything we face.

So many of us have become discouraged because we are not in control and we are powerless to do anything about what we face. Because God doesn't seem to be "showing up" when we think he should, we give up. The husband and wife who struggle with infertility wonder whether God has forgotten about them. The Christian stuck in a bad marriage wonders, "Will I ever see the power of God change my husband?" You could add to the list. But difficult, dark days are not an indication that God can't deal with what we're facing and that he has abandoned us.

God has many ways of delivering us and demonstrating his power. I think of Daniel's friends (Daniel 3), who refused to bow to worship the image that the Babylonian king, Nebuchadnezzar, had made. When the king made the statement, "And who is the god who will deliver you out of my hands?" (v. 15), Daniel's friends responded, "Our God whom we serve is able" (v. 17). They refused to question God's ability. They knew he was able.

Sometimes God chooses to demonstrate his power by supernaturally changing our circumstances. And sometimes he chooses to leave us in hard, difficult places, but gives us his sustaining power.

Look again at Romans 4:17, where Paul says that God "calls

into existence the things that do not exist." This puts Abraham and Sarah's dead situation in context. They were dealing with the Creator of the universe. The message: the One who had called all things into existence had the power to resurrect their "dead" situation and give them a baby, no matter how old they were.

How about you? Have you given up? Have you ever said to yourself, "This one just might be too big for God"? Or perhaps you're saying, "I'm growing weary, nothing has happened, and maybe it won't." But don't forget that the process is part of God's plan. As we wait for something to happen, we become something. We experience his transforming power.

### Strengthened

The fourth word is *strengthened*. More often than not, God's process is to make us strong through that which either threatens to destroy us or cannot be overcome in our own strength. Put another way, weakness and opposition are the pathway to strength and confidence.

Pay very close attention to what Paul says about the development of Abraham's faith in Romans 4:19–21: "He did not weaken in faith when he considered his own body, which was as good as dead . . . but . . . *grew strong* in his faith as he gave glory to God, fully convinced that God was able to do what he had promised."

A faith that is not tested is like a muscle that is not used. Both atrophy. Christianity is not simply a body of truth to be believed; it is a supernatural life that is meant to be lived. Our growth does not take place in the wonderful confines of our Bible studies, conferences, and fellowship groups. To be sure, we need these events and resources to encourage us. Our strength is found, however, in the heavy lifting of application. This has to happen when we are tested not only by the gap between our current reality and where God is calling us to be, but also when the winds of adversity are fiercely blowing against us.

Did you notice what Abraham did as he stared down the opposition? While he was waiting, "he gave glory to God" (v. 20). In context, this means that he kept worshiping God and acknowledging his awesome greatness and power. This active worship and ever-expanding vision of God began to transform Abraham even as he waited for God to come through. His worship produced strength and resolve. It placed the focus where it needed to be: on God and not on the opposition. The more he gave glory to God, the stronger his faith became. As Abraham waited, he worshiped. And the more he worshiped, the more the greatness and power of God gripped his being. Again, God changed Abraham before he changed Abraham's circumstances—so much so that he became "fully convinced that God was able to do what he had promised" (v. 21).

## LOOK TO GOD ALONE

Don't waste your waiting. The time between where we are and the fulfillment of the promise is designed to transform us. I want to encourage you to turn your waiting room into an altar or a tent of meeting. Take your fear, anxiety, and uncertainty to God our Father, the Ancient of Days. Pour out your heart before him and worship and praise him for who he is. You will find your faith and strength growing in proportion to your praise. The presence and power of God will become a deeply personal reality even before the miracle happens. Perhaps I should say that that *is* the miracle. On our way to receiving something, we become more than we had anticipated and our faith stronger than we thought possible. The test drives us to God, and in turn, he pours out his grace and strength on us.

When it comes to God, we never have to play it safe. He is not intimidated by anything we face. He can handle it, and then some. We get through and overcome not based on anything that we bring to the table. God, and God alone, is our strength and confidence.

## QUESTIONS FOR DISCUSSION OR REFLECTION

1. What does it mean to say that "our faith is a reflection of our view of God"? Do you agree?

2. Paul writes in 2 Corinthians 1:20, "For all the promises of God find their yes in [Christ]." What promises of God have been confirmed in your life?

3. Think of a time in your life when trusting God required defying your circumstances. If you are reading this book with others, share your experience with the group. If you are reading alone, write down the experience in a journal.

4. Abraham faced many obstacles as he walked toward the future God had for him. What part of Abraham's story resonates most with you?

# 2

# A Done Deal

The United States has had two presidents who were elected without opposition. George Washington was unopposed in 1789 and then again in 1792. Then there was James Monroe, who ran without opposition in 1820. Their "campaigns," such as they were, were mere formalities.

In the case of Washington, he simply had too much going for him. He had no peer. He was the face of the American Revolution and a war hero. He was a leader's leader. He was a living legend. I can imagine that every would-be opponent considered these advantages and concluded that it would border on being unpatriotic if not ridiculous to challenge him. Who in his right mind was going to run against George Washington? His position and place were secure.

In much the same way, our position and place as followers of Christ is secure and unshakeable. Nothing can pry us away from our Father's heart, our place in heaven, and his proactive, transforming love. This is the bedrock of our faith and confidence. This is not mere sentimentality, warm inspiring words devoid of power and life-sustaining meaning. No, our place and position in Christ means that we bring the very person of Christ and our security in him to all that we are, do and encounter. That's a very significant truth. We are not overmatched, outnumbered, and without resources.

Let these wonderful, celebratory words from Romans 8:31–39 wash over you and capture your heart and imagination:

> What then shall we say to these things? If God is for us, who can be against us? He who did not spare his own Son but gave him up for us all, how will he not also with him graciously give us all things? Who shall bring any charge against God's elect? It is God who justifies. Who is to condemn? Christ Jesus is the one who died—more than that, who was raised—who is at the right hand of God, who indeed is interceding for us. Who shall separate us from the love of Christ? Shall tribulation, or distress, or persecution, or famine, or nakedness, or danger, or sword? As it is written,
>
> > "For your sake we are being killed all the day long;
> > we are regarded as sheep to be slaughtered."
>
> No, in all these things we are more than conquerors through him who loved us. For I am sure that neither death nor life, nor angels nor rulers, nor things present nor things to come, nor powers, nor height nor depth, nor anything else in all creation, will be able to separate us from the love of God in Christ Jesus our Lord.

Let me suggest that you read the passage again, slowly and prayerfully. What unspeakable love. What confident assurance. What complete security.

One of my sweetest memories is of going to Yankee Stadium with my dad when I was a little boy. We began this tradition when I was about three or four. We would board the crowded train going up to the Bronx and walk through the throngs of people on our way to our seats. Pop would have his massive hand wrapped around mine, and sometimes he would reach down, pick me up, and carry me in his strong arms. I never was afraid when I was with my father. He was there. He would protect me. I was secure.

That's the point of Romans 8:31–39. God is there. He will protect us. We are secure.

This confidence, this security, is the foundation of our faith. In fact, there is no faith apart from the assurance of God's presence and, as we saw in the last chapter, the abiding, clear direction from his Word.

As we will see throughout this book, faith is not mere speculation, but it is embedded, anchored in our great, awesome God, who has come near through the person and work of his Son, our Savior, Jesus Christ. We are in Christ and Christ is in God. We are together for eternity. This means that every dream, circumstance, or challenge God gives us and allows to come our way is met by him. *He* is our eternal resource. *He* is with us. When we place our faith in him, he in turn releases to us the resources necessary to meet the need.

Paul wrote this paragraph at the end of Romans 8 to assure us that our victory in Christ is a done deal. His unconditional love is ours, and nothing can or will affect or alter his love for us. We don't have to earn God's love or fight to keep it. We have it.

Although there are seven questions in these verses, there are really three dominant, big questions. As we will see, these are rhetorical questions. The obvious answer to each of them is a resounding "No one" or "Nothing."

## THE SECURITY QUESTION

The first big question is, "If God is for us, who can be against us?" (v. 31). This is the security question. In other words, "Do I have what I need?" Of course the answer is, "Do I ever!" When we put the question in statement form, it becomes even more compelling: Since God is for us, no one can be against us. God never loses. He has no rivals. His resources are never depleted.

But you say, "That's God; what about me?" Remember, the point of this passage is that we are permanently held by God, and he does not forget, drop, or leave anyone who belongs to him. Again, verse 31 says that "*God* is for us." The issue is not who and what we are up against, but rather who is on our side.

I'm reminded of 2 Kings 6. The king of Syria was upset because Elisha the prophet was telling the king of Israel the whereabouts of the Syrian army. So the king of Syria sent "horses and chariots and a great army" (v. 14) to surround the city where Elisha lived. I suppose he thought, "I'm going to teach this little two-bit prophet not to mess with me." When Elisha's servant got up that morning and saw that massive Syrian army surrounding the city, he was petrified and wondered what in the world they were going to do. Then "Elisha prayed and said, 'O LORD, please open his eyes that he may see.' So the LORD opened the eyes of the young man, and he saw, and behold, the mountain was full of horses and chariots of fire all around Elisha" (vv. 17–18).

God gave Elisha's servant a glimpse of his supernatural resources and his protection. The battle was over before it started. Again, if God is for us, who can be against us?

There is a relationship between the depth and resiliency of our faith and our view of God. I sometimes think that in our desire to help people better "understand" God, we have reduced him to the level of our feeble definitions and made him too much like us. It is true that we are made in his image, but we mustn't make the mistake of remaking God into *our* image. He is beyond us and our comprehension. We approach God with great humility and awe because we know that he cannot be contained and he is totally other. This distance actually strengthens our faith, because we realize that he has what we don't, that he is what we are not, and that he loves us perfectly and unconditionally.

This God who is for us is all-knowing, all-powerful, everywhere present, unchanging and unchangeable, and self-existent. He is eternal. He is without need. He is just. He is righteous. He is merciful. He is holy. He is love. He is never without options. He doesn't need to consult with anyone about anything. He is the solution.

Yes, it is this God who is for us. And just in case we doubt the depth of his commitment to us, absorb the words of Romans 8:32: "He who did not spare his own Son but gave him up for us all, how will he not also with him graciously give us all things?" The message is that if God gave the best that he has, he is not going to hold back from us anything else we may need during our journey down here. It would be like paying thousands of dollars for a diamond ring and then arguing with the jeweler to give you the $5 box to put it in. That's silly.

We don't have to be rattled or intimidated. Just as a three-year-old boy held in the strong arms of his dad doesn't worry about his safety, we need not worry either, for God says to all of us, "You are in my hands." We need to shift our eyes from that which threatens to hurt or destroy us and focus instead on the Sustainer of the universe and the lover of our souls. He is not asleep or out of touch. He is for us and is here with us at this very moment. And he has everything we need and then some. Oh, if only we could see what Elisha's servant saw.

## THE LEGAL QUESTION

There's a second big question. Romans 8:33 says, "Who shall bring any charge against God's elect?" This is the legal question, which asks, "Am I guilty?"

My sisters and I grew up in a household in which family was a priority. Our parents were adamant that we were to support one another and be loyal to the members of our family. Many times when I was upset with my sisters or we were arguing about something, Pop would say: "You'd better remember that all you have in life is each other. That's your sister, son. Family. Work it out." We were blessed beyond measure to have parents who provided for us and protected us. There were several memorable times in my life when I saw my dad step forward and defend his family. Those actions said, loudly and clearly, "I will not let you or anyone else hurt or mistreat my family." Can you imagine the confidence this gave us? We were backed and supported.

This is the feeling, the spirit, of what Paul is saying in Romans 8:33–34. The key expression is "God's elect." The word *elect* means "chosen ones." We did not choose God and place ourselves in his family. No, *God* chose *us* and placed us in his family. He did it by purchasing us with the blood of his dear Son. He sought us. He found us. He saved us. He sustains us. He will bring us into his presence. We are members of his family, and he lovingly and tenaciously watches over us. To be a member of the family of God means to be secure and confident. We take bold steps of faith because we know who is with us, who supports us, and who fights our battles.

But there is something more specific that Paul wants us to understand and embrace. As God's elect, we are not guilty, we are not condemned. The charges cannot stick. Here he is referring to both our sinful condition and the sins that we have committed, both of which had not only separated us from God but assigned us to eternal condemnation. But now, through faith in Christ, we are not guilty. Thus, the guilt-erasing, soul-liberating statement in Romans 8:1: "There is therefore now no condemnation for those who are in Christ Jesus."

Formal charges can no longer be made against God's elect. Please read that sentence again. That's right, formal charges cannot be made against God's elect. If you have trusted Christ as your Savior and Lord, you are not condemned. We are free to enjoy him, to live for him, and to confidently trust him to meet our every need.

As a pastor, I have counseled countless people who struggle with the assurance of their salvation. And the shrapnel of doubt is embedded in their entire approach to the Christian life, leaving gaping holes in their confidence and their ability to have a certain, sure walk with Christ. Typically the angst and uncertainty tends to fall under the banner of one of two questions. The first is, "How can God ever forgive me for the awful things I've done?" This is self-punishment and the refusal to accept the unconditional forgiveness of God secured once and for all through the death of Christ on the cross. The second question is something like this: "How do I know that I really, sincerely placed my faith in Christ?" This question launches people on an agonizing downward spiral of one negative "what if" scenario after another, sometimes leading to depression and a paralyzing hopelessness. Again, obviously, without assurance there is no confidence and no possibility of exercising life-transforming, event-altering faith.

So what do I tell them? Often I point them to this very passage, for it speaks to our guilt and the nature of our salvation.

Look again at verse 33 and pay close attention to the short, powerful answer Paul gives to his question: "Who shall bring any charge against God's elect? *It is God who justifies.*" To be justified means to be declared righteous. Paul refers to this declaration of righteousness when he says in Romans 5:1, "Therefore, since we have been justified by faith, we have peace with God through our Lord Jesus Christ." When we turn to Christ, we are declared righteous in the sight of God, and that brings peace between us and him.

But God is the One who justifies us, who declares us righteous. That does not mean that God somehow ignores our sin, that he is living in denial about what we are really like. No, God never overlooks sin. He knows and has seen every nasty, filthy thing we have done. He is very much aware of our selfishness and sinful actions. He knows the sinful secrets of our hearts and the dark cracks and crevices where we not only have allowed our minds to visit but to take up residence. We have angered him. We have hurt his heart. We have willfully and willingly disobeyed him. God knows this and more.

Yet he justifies us. Why? Because he loves us and he knows that we are utterly helpless and completely powerless to change our condition or even come close to meeting his standard, which is perfection. So God provided his own solution to our sin and guilt, Jesus Christ, the Lamb of God, who takes away the sin of the world (John 1:29). God could declare us righteous because his own Son satisfied the requirements of his holiness. That's what John means when he says in 1 John 2:2, "He [Jesus] is the propitiation [satisfaction] for our sins, and not for ours only but also for the sins of the whole world."

You see, when we understand that we did not provide for or participate in our salvation, but that God did it all for us, we are filled with wonder, worship, and a sense of profound gratitude. Yes, we were guilty, but he paid the price to declare us righteous. What God has said and done stands. Don't be distracted by the accusations from Satan, others, or even yourself. Dismiss them. They are empty and cannot alter in the least our eternal destination and position in Christ. The moment we turned from our sin to Christ, we were declared righteous.

This means that our sin has been expunged from our record.

A friend told me that his daughter had been caught speeding. She was going 30 miles per hour over the speed limit, and the officer had no mercy on her. Her driver's license was suspended. However, she was told that if she went to driving school, she would get her license back, and if she didn't get any more speeding tickets for a year, the ticket would be expunged from her record. In other words, her record would be wiped clean. That was a no-brainer. She went to the classes. She got her license back. She drove within the speed limit. Now, there is no record anywhere of her speeding violation. It cannot be found.

When Christ died on the cross, that's what happened to our sins. No one can condemn us, because Christ died for our sins. That's what Paul says in Romans 8:34: "Who is to condemn? Christ Jesus is the one who died—more than that, who was raised—who is at the right hand of God, who is indeed interceding for us." When Christ died, our sin and guilt were transferred to him. That's the point of 2 Corinthians 5:21: "For our sake he made him to be sin who knew no sin, so that in him we might become the righteousness of God." I love the description in Colossians 2:13–14: "And you, who were dead in your trespasses and the uncircumcision of your flesh, God made alive together with him, having forgiven us all our trespasses, by canceling the record of debt that stood against us with its legal demands. This he set aside, nailing it to the cross."

What does this mean? When we trust Christ, we experience full forgiveness, the complete removal of our offenses and guilt. When others search our records, all they can see is red—the blood of Christ covering our sin. Not only that, the Bible teaches that Jesus currently stands before God the Father as our Advocate, declaring that his death on the cross has paid for our sins (1 John 2:1). We are clean and we are free.

Because the verdict is in—not guilty—there is no barrier between us and God. What others say doesn't matter. Again, their charges and accusations are empty and cannot stick. We're no longer held hostage to the sins and the guilt of our past. This means that we are free to trust God. We are in his family and he is our loving heavenly Father, who cares for us and has promised to meet our every need. We can take bold, confident steps of faith.

Just in case we're wondering how secure our place is in God's family, Paul reminds us that we are permanent, eternal members of it. Our acceptance is unconditional. There is no sixty-day probationary period in which we have to demonstrate that we are worthy of his love, and if we don't quite measure up, we'll get cut loose.

God will not change his mind. Our inconsistencies, weaknesses, and failures not only won't but can't get us booted out of the family. Our own children can hurt us and disappoint us, but we can't biologically disown them. They can't become "unborn" and shed our genes. So it is with our relationship with God. Once we experience the new birth, we cannot become "unborn" (John 3:1–18; Titus 3:4–8). We are his forever. And that's because it is God who justifies.

## THE RELATIONSHIP QUESTION

So, then, we have the third big question: "Who shall separate us from the love of Christ?" (Rom. 8:35). This is the relationship question. In other words, "Will I be abandoned?" The answer is a resounding, emphatic no. Nothing or no one can separate us from him.

These verses are like the grand climax of George Frideric

Handel's *Messiah*. I'm convinced that when Paul wrote these words, he intended for them to be read with passion, volume, and great confidence—just as Handel intended for his "Hallelujah Chorus." God's love through Christ holds us permanently in his family. Believe it. Declare it. Celebrate it. And live confidently based upon it.

Notice, it is not our love for Christ that gives us our security. No, verse 35 says it is the "love *of* Christ" that holds us. This love, which belongs to and originates from Christ, is pure, consistent, unaffected, and permanent. It is anchored in Christ and not in us, and that's the reason why no one or nothing can separate us from it.

Literally nothing or no one can separate us from the love of Christ. Paul mentions the ultimate threats in verse 38. Death cannot and will not affect the love of Christ for us because we have the gift of eternal life. Death has been defeated at the cross and through the resurrection. Therefore, death is not final, but merely the transition into the presence of God (Phil. 1:21–23).

Likewise, life cannot affect the love of Christ for us. This refers to the tragic twists and turns in life. In other words, nothing we will ever encounter in life is strong enough to pry us away from the eternal grip of God's love through Christ. It cannot happen.

Supernatural powers cannot separate us from the love of Christ. Romans 8:38 says, "nor angels nor rulers, nor things present nor things to come, nor powers . . ." We are followers of Christ and members of his family. There is no power, no Devil or demon, no "powerful" person, no set of circumstances, and no issue in life that can separate us from the love of Christ. Whatever happens tomorrow ("things to come") or next year, for that matter, cannot change or affect in any way the love of Christ for us.

This incomparable, incomprehensible eternal love is not only our security and comfort; it is our victory. That's what Paul says in verse 37: "No, in all these things we are more than conquerors through him who loved us." Notice, our victory is found in and through the One who loves us. He secured our victory at the cross and continues to lead us in victory on a daily basis. It is not God's will that we "just get by" and "barely make it" as his followers. No, we are "more than conquerors." That's because we are in Christ, and what he has is made available to us (Eph. 1:3–14). His love is not just a sentimental love, but a transforming, empowering love. It is ours. Believe it. Live in it. Live on it. Watch the Savior work.

Because we are secure ("God is for us"), because we are no longer guilty ("Who shall bring any charge against God's elect?"), and because we will never be abandoned ("Who shall separate us from the love of Christ?"), we are confident. The assurance question is taken off the table. God is with us, so we are free to exercise focused, believing faith.

## QUESTIONS FOR DISCUSSION OR REFLECTION

1. Do you feel secure in Christ's love? Or do you fear you will lose his approval if you don't do, say, or believe the right things? Take a few moments to read and reflect on Romans 8:38–39.

2. What would it be like if you concentrated on God's sufficiency, instead of your insufficiency, in the midst of a current struggle?

3. Take a moment to read 2 Kings 6:14–18. Do you struggle to believe that God has resources available for you, even when you cannot see them?

4. Have you ever forgiven someone who struggled to feel forgiven by you? How did that make you feel?

5. Our confidence comes from what God has done, not what we do or have done. How would you summarize in your own words what God has accomplished for you?

# 3

# The Certainty of Our Future

Some people are thrill seekers, who put their lives on the line in exchange for the euphoric feeling of having teased death and "won." You've seen them. They include the guy who walks across the Grand Canyon on a wire. They are motorcycle riders who drive up ramps at top speed just to see if they can jump over a string of tractor-trailers parked side by side. Then there's the guy who gets dropped off in some wilderness for a week in subzero temperatures, surrounded by hungry, vicious predators, with only the clothes on his back and a knife in his pocket.

Although many people are attracted to the suspense that comes from watching these "death-defying" feats (check the television ratings!), most of us are not willing to try anything like these stunts. We like life and we like living. We figure that there is too much at stake; we would rather choose certainty over uncertainty. We like the assurance that, all things being equal, we will wake up in the morning and still be here for our families and make our 10 a.m. meetings. So there's some stuff that we are not willing to do or risk.

But there are no guarantees. Life itself is uncertain. You may be a disciplined, meticulous planner with the resources and relationships to provide you with options and contingencies that others simply don't have. But sooner or later, all of us will be thrown into the darkness of uncertainty and be reminded again that even on our best days, we are dependent people. We need a hope and assurance that, frankly, eclipses anything that we bring to the table.

This is where I live.

As a pastor, I am called to help others find their way through the haze of uncertainty. Plans and dreams are interrupted by the unanticipated: the death of a family member; the sudden loss of a job; the diagnosis of cancer; the surprise moral "meltdown" of a teenager; the revelation that a spouse has been unfaithful; and the general bizarre combination of life's unforeseen challenges and circumstances.

Fear and uncertainty visit us. The future is put on hold. This is not according to the plan. Not only do we not know what to do next, we don't know what's going to happen next. The haze has set in. Faith is being challenged and tested in real time. It's not someone else's future that's in jeopardy; it's ours. We feel the darkness closing in on us, so we search for hope and reassurance. We are struggling; at best, we find ourselves identifying with the man who said to Jesus, "I believe; help my unbelief!" (Mark 9:24).

But uncertainty is a gift from God. Dark, uncertain times can either drive us to despair or point us to the One who knows and holds our future. When we turn to God, we have chosen the path of faith.

You see, faith is born, tested, and developed during the darkness of uncertainty. Faith and self-reliance cannot occupy the same space. So in order to strengthen our faith, God removes our resources and allows us to enter the dark valley of uncertainty. This valley is not always about suffering and hardship; sometimes it's about the delays and detours of our dreams and plans.

In this valley, our great God poses a question to us: "Are you still going to believe me?" In other words, are we going to keep walking toward God? Christian thinker and revivalist A. W. Tozer said, "Christian faith is not so much what you say you believe, but how you behave in a consistent manner."[4] In this regard, *faith* is a verb even though it's a noun. In other words, faith is not faith if there is no action. We keep believing God, exercising faith, even when we don't see resolution.

That's what Hebrews 11:1–12:3 is all about. In this chapter and the next three, I want to point to and draw out the rich, wonderful lessons about faith that we can learn from the men and women of God mentioned in this compelling portion of Scripture. They pressed through their dark, uncertain times. It is my prayer that their journeys of faith will pour fresh encouragement and holy motivation into our hearts and souls.

Let me encourage you to put this book down, pick up your Bible, and read Hebrews 11:1–12:3. Please read this passage slowly and prayerfully. You may want to read it twice.

Notice that various forms of the word *commend* (English Standard Version) are used five times in Hebrews 11 (vv. 2, 4, 5, 39). The Greek word for "commend" is *martyreō*, from which we get the English word *martyr*. The word means to "bear witness." But the way the word is used in Hebrews 11 does not mean that our faith witnesses to God, but that God witnesses on our behalf because we are exercising faith. It's as if God says:

"Look at my children. Despite what they are going through, they believe me and trust me." God is cheering us on.

Our two sons were both athletes. Bryan played football and basketball, and Bryndan played baseball. I loved watching them play, and obviously I was thrilled when their teams won. But I always watched more intently when, in the middle of a game, the pressure was on and they were faced with the choice of caving in to the opposition or reaching down deep and giving it all that they had. As a dad, I was most proud when they didn't pull back in the heat of battle or let their teams down by caving in to fear. At the end of each game, we would hug and celebrate.

In much the same way, when we don't shrink back because of opposition, delays, and disappointments, God celebrates our faith. He cheers us on. He rewards us. He points to us as examples and models of enduring faith.

It is my view that this section of Scripture is about the *motivation* for an enduring faith. Hebrews 11 begins with a stated focus (vv. 1–3), and the thought/discussion comes to a compelling climax in Hebrews 12:1–3. Sandwiched between the focus and the outcome are biographical snapshots of men and women of God who refused to quit, but instead kept believing God to make tangible what they knew was a reality in their hearts. In short, when confronted with the challenge of uncertainty, these pilgrims put one foot in front of the other and moved with certainty toward the fulfillment of the promise. This is what we call faith.

The two big reasons why we, too, should keep moving are given to us in verses 1–3 and then in verse 6 of chapter 11. First, faith expresses our security (vv. 1–3). Second, faith magnifies and expresses our holy ambition (v. 6).

Hebrews 11:1–3 reads: "Now faith is the assurance of things hoped for, the conviction of things not seen. For by it the people of old received their commendation. By faith we understand that the universe was created by the word of God, so that what is seen was not made out of things that are visible."

This is a description of what faith does and how it works. Before giving us the profiles in faith that dominate the rest of chapter 11, the writer wants to make a strong, clear statement. Here it is: *faith frees us from the fear of the future.*

Let's face it, uncertainty has a way of slowing our pace, if not paralyzing us altogether. When we are uncertain, we no longer run the race with courage and focus. We are timid, distracted, and, in a word, insecure.

However, Hebrews 11 is showing us the *concreteness of faith*. It is described as "the assurance of things hoped for." This faith is sure. Faith is to a Christian what a foundation is to a house. It gives us stability and confidence. Further, the word *assurance* can be taken to mean the title deed for what we are believing God to do. The fact that God has placed faith in your heart to believe him for something that currently does not exist is the title deed for its existence.

This passage also shows us the *certainty of faith*. It is further described as "the conviction of things not seen." The word *conviction* has to do with the state of being persuaded or convinced.

But there is a tension here. How do we know that what we are believing God for will happen? Can we exercise faith and be wrong? The short answer is yes. We will never talk God into doing something that he does not want done. We can claim it, talk as if it has already happened, and make plans based upon our "positive" declaration, and be wrong the whole time.

Not every idea, dream, or desire that I have had through the years and for which I exercised faith has come to reality. There was the new building that never happened. There was the conference that never got off the ground. There was the ministry opportunity that didn't work out.

At this point, you're probably thinking: "Crawford, it sounds as if you are contradicting what you just said. If it is possible to exercise faith and be wrong, how can faith be 'the conviction of things not seen'?"

I have learned some hard but very important lessons along these lines. Specifically, I have learned that there are biblical principles that should trigger and govern the expression and exercise of our faith. *Faith is the response to what God wants done and is initiating in and through our lives.* So when a desire or an idea visits me, before I head off in the "faith" direction, I've learned to ask these five questions:

1. *Is there any unconfessed sin in my life?* Faith has no integrity and is powerless apart from holiness. God is not into compartmentalization. We can believe God for the right thing but have a wrong heart, in which case our faith is meaningless. A clean heart gives weight to our faith.

2. *Is this idea or desire anchored in the Word of God?* God is not a part of anything that contradicts his Word. To say that we are exercising faith in God for something that his Word is against is self-deception and manipulation. It won't work.

3. *Is this idea or desire intensified when I pray?* If, when we pray, the desire will not release us, then this may very well be God's call to release our faith in its direction.

4. *Is the witness of the Holy Spirit affirming the idea or desire on my heart?* The Holy Spirit leads and guides us to the things God has for us and wants to do through us

during our journey. He will lead us if we are yielded to him and listening.

5. *Does this idea or desire pass the wisdom test?* I have found that the insights and perspectives of wise, godly people are more often than not used of God to bring clarity and affirmation to the path and direction of my faith.

Holiness, the Word of God, prayer, the leading of the Holy Spirit, and the counsel of wise, godly people inform, affirm, and confirm our faith. These factors take it out of the realm of hopeful speculation and translate it to confident certainty. It becomes the assurance of things hoped for and the conviction of things not seen.

We are also a part of the *community of faith*. Verse 2 says, "For by it the people of old received their commendation." The rest of Hebrews 11 is application of this verse. Once again, keep in mind that faith brings the attention and applause of heaven. As we will see later, faith is not always recognized and rewarded in this life or in our generation. But it is always recognized and rewarded by God ("commendation"). We are not alone. We are newcomers to a long line of faith-filled pilgrims ("the people of old"), who marked their moments in history by trust in the unfailing God. Faith is both our heritage and our legacy. Our heritage is what we receive and our legacy is what we leave. Those who came before us have placed faith in our hands; we will place the treasure of our faith in the hands of the next generation. The saints of old bridged the gaps between where they were and what God was calling them to be and to do, and as we look back, it's as if they are cheering us on, saying: "Press on, keep believing. God did it for us and he will do it for you."

This leads to the *continuity of faith* in verse 3. The writer points to creation as an illustration of God's track record of calling things into existence. Look at the line "so that what is seen was not made out of things that are visible." The fact that we can't see our way clear does not mean that God cannot make the way clear. Just because you don't have what you need and can't see how you are going to get it doesn't mean that God won't give it to you. The author is making the point that God is in the business of making the invisible visible. God has not changed. Creation is an illustration of how he works in and through his people throughout history. In other words, just as God spoke the world into existence, so he uses our faith to bring into existence that which he places on our hearts. Faith is spiritual creation.

## FAITH MAGNIFIES AND EXPRESSES OUR HOLY AMBITION

Hebrews 11:6 reads, "And without faith it is impossible to please him, for whoever would draw near to God must believe that he exists and that he rewards those who seek him."

This is a very strong, focused statement. The writer assumes that it is the desire of every follower of Christ to please God. In 2 Corinthians 5:9, the apostle Paul puts it this way: "We make it our aim to please [the Lord]." And Hebrews 11:6 tells us what pleases him: faith. God commends us for our faith because he is pleased when we trust him. Faith is an expression of our ambition to please God. In other words, when we choose faith over fear and uncertainty, we declare our allegiance to God and our desire to honor and glorify him. When we do that, God is pleased.

We all know what it is like not to be believed or trusted. It's not only disappointing, it's insulting. It is especially painful when you have acted with pure motives and consistently followed through on your commitments and promises. Yet that track record is ignored, and the person or group you are trying to serve maligns your integrity by choosing not to believe that you will stand on and by your word. You're left scratching your head and wondering, "What more do I need to do to demonstrate that I'm trustworthy?"

Can you imagine how God must feel when we reject his track record and choose self-reliance or doubt and unbelief over faith? He is insulted and not pleased.

To be sure, if we are followers of Christ, we definitely don't want to attack God's integrity. But fear has a way of shifting our focus away from God and onto our circumstances. Fear nudges us toward disobedience, and in our "nervous condition," we either give up or take the reins and attempt to do what only God can do. God is not pleased, and we are left frustrated and defeated.

We were not born to be self-reliant. We were born to live a life that is dependent on God and to experience and express his plan and purposes for our lives during our moment in history. To choose not to exercise faith is to choose not to please God ("without faith it is *impossible* to please him"). Again, God is glorified when we trust him. Our faith pleases God, and the joy and pleasure of God is our holy ambition.

The second part of verse 6 calls for a foundational, fundamental decision. In fact, this is a call to make a historic, permanent decision concerning who God is and what he does. You might think that that sentence is a bit over the top. You know how it goes—make an excessive statement in order to make a point. But I can assure you that is not the case in this instance.

Look at the word *believe*. Now bear with me as I dig into the technicalities. This word is a verb, and in the Greek text, it is in what is known as the aorist tense. The aorist tense differs from the past tense in that it points not just to a past action, but to a decisive, historic action that is to be viewed as a point of reference and not something to be repeated. It points to a defining moment or event that changes the trajectory of the events that follow, a benchmark decision that one henceforth lives and functions in light of.

A great example of this is found in Romans 12:1. Here Paul charges us to "present [our] bodies as a living sacrifice." The verb *present* is in the aorist tense. The message is that we mustn't vacillate as to whether or not we're going to be living sacrifices. We must make the decision and live accordingly. Put another way, if I make that decision, I am accountable to live in that direction.

On May 22, 1971, Karen and I exchanged vows and entered into a lifelong covenant called marriage. It was a historic event that changed every other relationship in our lives. Everything changed. Two people became one, and we live life based upon that reality. We face decisions and see relationships and responsibilities in light of our marriage covenant.

In much the same way, we must make the definitive decision that God is real ("exists") and that he is for us and will respond to us if we pursue him ("rewards those who seek him").

Put another way, our actions declare what we have decided to believe about God. The strength of our faith is not determined by what we go through or by what we face. The strength of our faith is seen, proved, and demonstrated based upon what we have decided to believe about God before we enter the fire. We must make up our minds that God's existence is not theoretical or distant. He is here. He is near. He is with us every moment and every second of every day, no matter what. And this very God is not impotent or threatened by anything that we face or experience. The outcome and the victory do not depend on our strength and resources. This ever-present God whispers in our ears, "If you turn to me and seek me, I will give you everything that you need to break through what stands before you." But again, we must settle in our minds that we will believe, we will trust, and we will turn to him.

Let me suggest seven keys to strengthening your faith. Here's the list:

1. Accept the reality of opposition. There is no such thing as faith unless there is opposition.
2. Stand ready to resist. We have a real enemy (Satan) who uses uncertainty and opposition to move us toward unbelief.
3. Keep your mind focused and filled with truth. We must discipline ourselves to read, study, memorize, and meditate on God's Word. It is the fuel for our faith.
4. Embrace the growth pains. Our faith grows in proportion to the challenges that we face. Don't run from a challenge; instead, turn to God and allow him to "grow" you in it.
5. Stay in God's presence. Develop a heart that pursues holiness and worship. He promises his favor to those who seek him.
6. Associate with faith-filled people. Critical, negative, carnal Christians dismantle and drain the faith out of the best of us. Avoid them and associate with followers of Christ who will point you toward God's sufficiency.
7. Act. Faith is not for discussion groups or Bible studies. Faith is something that we do.

The strength does not reside in us; it is in him. Are you weary, beaten down, worn out, and confused? Do you feel as if you are being swept away or swallowed up by the challenges in front of you? That there's no more fight in you? That you've come to the end of yourself? It is OK to doubt ourselves and to question our abilities and the adequacy of our resources. In fact, God has orchestrated the contrast to remind us that the battle is not ours; it is his. Again, it is not the strength of our faith, but the power and sufficiency of our great God that makes the difference. It is not what we have, but who we turn to and what he has that matters. Doubt yourself, but don't doubt him. Believe and turn to him. Open your hands and your heart, and he will fill them.

## QUESTIONS FOR DISCUSSION OR REFLECTION

1. Can you recall a time when a period of uncertainty led you into greater faith? Tell the story to your group or write about it in your journal.

2. From time to time, each of us becomes convinced that a dream or goal is from the Lord. How do you normally determine if a desire in your heart was put there by God or by yourself?

3. Can you recall a time when someone didn't trust you, even when you had been trustworthy? How did that make you feel?

4. Take a look at your life. What does your behavior communicate about your view of God? Is your life a testimony to your confidence in God?

5. What one positive step can you take to better demonstrate your faith in God's sufficiency?

# 4

# Faith Is Obedience

Some years ago, when I was on the U.S. leadership team of Cru (formerly Campus Crusade for Christ), we went on a retreat in the High Sierras in Northern California. The goal of our time together was to enhance our unity as a team. We did a number of team-building exercises, including rappelling 200 feet straight down the face of a natural rock "wall." You entrusted your life to two guys at the top, who were holding your rope as you "bounced off" the wall on your way to the ground below. As I looked at my two colleagues, I was tempted to fake a panic attack or at least ask if I could pass on this particular exercise. It was one thing to say that I trusted these guys, but it was quite another to look at them holding the rope in their hands and act on that trust by pushing off and descending to the ground while believing that they would not let me go. Finally, I pushed off and they didn't let me go. I made it down, safe and sound.

Remember, *faith* is a verb even though it is a noun. In order for faith to be faith, there must be action. For example, Colossians 2:6 says, "Therefore, as you received Christ Jesus the Lord, so walk in him." How did we receive Christ? It wasn't by intellectual assent or through dialoguing with other Christians. We became followers of Christ when we turned to him from our sin and believed in our hearts that his death on the cross was sufficient to establish a relationship with God. We trusted (faith) him with our lives and our eternal futures. We acted.

This same faith principle is to govern every aspect of our lives ("so walk in him"). This is what the Bible means when it says, "We walk by faith, not by sight" (2 Cor. 5:7). To live by faith is more than a suggestion in the Bible; it is a command. Therefore, living by faith is an act of obedience. Once again, it is not just a frame of mind; it is a willful choice to turn to God as our source and sufficiency to meet every need and challenge we have—whether it is expressing our faith in him to heal a sick child, to give us the money to pay our bills, to change the heart and life of a spouse, or to fulfill a dream or a calling he has placed on our heart. In all of these circumstances, when we choose faith over doubt, we are choosing obedience over disobedience.

There are three spheres in which we must exercise this obedient faith. The first is the sphere of complete, unreserved obedience to the Word of God. We believe it and act on it. The second sphere is the assignments God brings to us and calls us to. We trust him and follow his leading without reservation. The third sphere is the challenges, trials, needs, and gaps in our lives. We trust him for his provision and intervention. God has called us to obedience in each sphere.

There are very serious consequences when, in disobedience, we choose not to exercise faith. Not the least of these is the danger of becoming stuck in a lifeless complacency, barricading ourselves from the transforming, life-giving favor and pleasure of God, and missing the joy of knowing and experiencing his plan for our lives. Yes, choosing not to exercise faith is always more convenient than trusting what we can't see or quantify.

However, keep in mind that faith is obedience, and disobedience is always far more expensive than obedience.

As we will see, living by faith is not always an easy obedience. Faith is a scary, risky business. For most of us, it can be a very uncomfortable obedience. But every follower of Christ without exception is called to the adventure of experiencing and developing an obedient faith.

Faith forces issues and decisions. Faith exposes reality and demands an answer to the question: "Are you going to trust what you can see and what your current resources can handle, or are you going to respond in obedience to what God has placed on your heart to do, become, and receive?" Action is the great truth-teller and barometer of our faith.

Karen and I have been on this faith journey the entire forty-three years of our marriage. Every ministry assignment we have had and every dilemma and need that has confronted us has been a test of obedience. As we look back over our journey, we are struck by how God has dealt with us. It's as if he has said to us: "I'm going to show you enough for you to know that I am leading you, but I'm not going to give you what you need before you obey me. First you act, then you will receive. If you receive before you act, you will trust the resource and not the source—me."

We didn't have everything we "needed" when we left the security of Philadelphia and moved to Dallas to plant a church. We didn't have everything we "needed" when we joined the staff of Cru. We didn't have everything we "needed" to pay the college tuition for four kids. We didn't have everything we "needed" when we left Cru and I became the senior pastor of Fellowship Bible Church. The same is true for all of the crises and trials we have had and will continue to face along our journey.

God has met every need and bridged every gap. Vision has been translated to reality, we have experienced the supernatural intervention and provision of God in ways that take our breath away, and our children have gone to college and graduate school without the anchor of indebtedness. God has reminded us time and again that this is all because our response to him was obedient action. It is depressing to think about what we would have missed by choosing a "comfortable" disobedience over risky faith. Along the way, we have learned, sometimes the hard way, that regret is the product of not responding in faith. So with an elevated heart rate and nervous steps, we moved ahead on the path of faith.

## FAITH EXHIBIT A: ABRAHAM

This is not unlike Abraham. He too stepped away from a predictable life onto the path of faith. In fact, when we consider that faith is obedience, Abraham's life is exhibit A. Hebrews 11:8–12, 17–19 describes his responsive, obedient faith:

> By faith Abraham obeyed when he was called to go out to a place that he was to receive as an inheritance. And he went out, not knowing where he was going. By faith he went to live in the land of promise, as in a foreign land, living in tents with Isaac and Jacob, heirs with him of the same promise. For he was looking forward to the city that has foundations, whose designer and builder is God. By faith Sarah herself received power to conceive, even when she was past the age, since she considered him faithful who had promised. Therefore from one man, and him as good as dead, were born descendants as many as the stars of heaven and as many as the innumerable grains of sand by the seashore. . . .
>
> By faith Abraham, when he was tested, offered up Isaac, and he who had received the promises was in the act of

offering up his only son, of whom it was said, "Through Isaac shall your offspring be named." He considered that God was able even to raise him from the dead, from which, figuratively speaking, he did receive him back.

This is a compelling picture of the relationship between faith and obedience. Every time Abraham responded to God in faith, he was sending a message to himself and those watching him: "I choose to obey God over against my circumstances and the uncertainty of the future." There are some rich, transforming implications in this story for all of us.

### The Unknown Destination

First, Abraham teaches us *to bey God when we don't know where we are going.* God did not tell Abraham where exactly he was to go. Still, when God spoke, Abraham acted: "And he went out, not knowing where he was going" (v. 8). No destination was specified and nothing was said about how long it would take to get there. Abraham had no idea what he would encounter along the way. He just knew that God had said to go, so he did.

I don't know about you, but most of the time I wish God would give me more information so that I could be better prepared for what's in front of me. That way, I could think through my options and contingencies, and make sure that I have all of the resources that I need. I can't help but think I would be more confident and make better decisions and choices if I knew what to anticipate.

But perhaps that's the problem. Planning is not wrong, and in fact, the Bible celebrates planning and says that it is wise and good. But a problem arises when we place our trust in anything or anyone over God—including our plans. We deceive ourselves into thinking that we are being "prudent" and rational stewards of our lives and resources when in fact we simply want to be in control. In truth, we often focus on planning because we are immobilized by fear. Fear wears many disguises, including what appears to be wisdom.

Years ago, a friend told me that he believed God was calling him to pursue full-time vocational ministry, but he wanted to make sure that he was ready for the move before he acted. From time to time, I checked in with him to see if there was any way I could be of help or encouragement to him. I noticed a pattern in our conversations. Each time I asked him when he was going to pull the trigger and make the move, he would say to me: "I'm waiting on the Lord. I don't want to get ahead of him." After the third or fourth time he said this to me, I asked him, "Are you sure God is telling you to wait or are you afraid to move?"

God wants us to apply wisdom to every choice and decision in life. But to respond to God before having all of the information we think we need may not be foolish at all. Wisdom does not mean that we have all of the answers, so that we know the "what" and "how" of our future. Wisdom means that we respond in a godly way to whatever we are faced with and wherever God is taking us. We can use (or misuse) Bible verses to rationalize ourselves into a comfortable, stagnant disobedience. Thus, the wisest thing to do is to obey God, as Abraham did, even when we don't know where we are going.

If we demand to have all of the answers before we act, we are saying to God that he has to trust us before we move. But when we act on what God has made clear, we are saying that we submit to his sovereign control over our lives and that we trust him. This is the heart of the matter. God withholds information from us in order for us to demonstrate his lordship over the affairs of our lives. So this is a control issue. In other words, when we exercise this kind of obedient faith, it is an act of surrender. We are saying we don't need to know *where* God is taking us; we just need to know that God *is* taking us.

When our kids were growing up, Karen and I learned early on that there was a point at which answering every "why" question they had concerning our decisions and directives as their parents was unhealthy. Doing so erodes authority and amounts to a reversal of roles. It would have launched them down a path of entitlement. There are times when parents need to answer the "why" question by saying, "Because I said so, and I expect you to fully comply with what I just said, end of discussion." This is not to be cruel or unnecessarily heavy-handed. We simply know things that our children don't know and see things that they don't see. So it's more important for them to trust us and respond to us than it is for them to have all of the answers.

When God called Abraham to go, that meant he had to leave home. Genesis 12:1 says, "Now the LORD said to Abram, 'Go from your country and your kindred and your father's house to the land that I will show you.'" The charge and the challenge was to leave certainty for uncertainty. Abraham was called to leave that which he was sure about to pursue and experience a promise that he would eventually realize. He could not go where God was leading him and stay within the comfort and confines of what he knew and loved. As a very dear friend of mine says, "You can't go with God and stay where you are."

But why did Abraham leave? The short answer, is because he knew, loved, and trusted God. He loved God more than he did his family, friends, and country. Faith is the manifestation of our walk and relationship with God. If we know him, we will trust him. If we trust him, we will follow him by faith, even if it means letting go and walking away from what is dear to us.

Over the years, I have talked to the parents of missionaries who are serving in some fairly hostile, dangerous places around the world. I sometimes ask them how they are handling the separation from their children and, in some cases, their grandchildren. I often hear something like this: "We miss them a lot. But we would rather have them far away doing what God has called them to do than for them to be close by but disobedient and out of God's will." That is a wonderful attitude.

An obedient faith says that we are unattached and ready to move. In Hebrews 11:9, we have a picture of Abraham living in *tents*. Abraham had to be flexible and mobile in order to move toward the promise. He didn't build a compound. He had to be ready to move whenever God spoke.

That's the point. In the words of George Morrison, "The important thing is not what we live in, but what we look for."[5] Faith says we are ready and willing to obey God and go where he leads, even when we don't know where that is. God is writing his statement through our lives during our moment in history. We can play it safe and make assumptions about God and his plan for our lives, or choose to take steps of faith-filled obedience toward the fulfillment of that which he places before us and in our hearts.

### The Uncertain Timetable

Second, Abraham teaches us *to obey God even when we don't know when God will fulfill his promise.*

In chapter 1, I emphasized the humanly impossible challenge and predicament in which Abraham and Sarah found themselves. They were many years past the ability to have children;

nevertheless, God said that they would have a child. And eventually they did. In Hebrews 11:11, we read about the fulfillment of that promise: "By faith Sarah herself received power to conceive, even when she was past the age, since she considered him faithful who had promised."

The time between God's promise of a son and the birth of Isaac was filled with tension and disobedience for Abraham and Sarah (Genesis 15–21). They grew impatient. Sarah encouraged Abraham to sleep with her servant, Hagar, and he agreed. Hagar became pregnant. Sarah got angry and jealous, and evidently did some very mean things to Hagar ("Sarah dealt harshly with her," Gen. 16:6). Hagar ran away, but the angel of the Lord sent her back (v. 9). Ishmael was born, but he wasn't the one God had promised to Abraham and Sarah. That was a very costly act of disobedience.

I can imagine the conversation between them: "Look, I know God promised to give us a son, but look at us. It hasn't happened yet, and given our condition, it is not going to happen via the conventional route. Perhaps God wants us to more broadly interpret what he said. After all, time is running out." Ouch! They had to learn that faith is not only obeying when you don't know *where* you are going; it is also waiting when you don't know *when* God is going to act or move. Sometimes it takes more faith to stand still than it does to move forward. This too is obedience.

As it did for Abraham and Sarah, impatience can cause us to make some bad assumptions and create some messes along the way. It is a bit painful for me to write these words, because I have struggled with patience my entire life. In recent years, I have made progress, but I still have a ways to go. God has been teaching me that I am not to create his next move for me, but to wait on him to show me not only what to do next but when to do it. Impatience causes us to take on too much work, to move too fast and too soon, and to assume more responsibility than we should. And if we're in positions of leadership or influence, others have to pay the tab for our impatient choices and decisions. That certainly happened with regard to Abraham and Sarah's "quick fix" substitute—Hagar—for God's provision. The result? Relational shrapnel in the family and the seeds of turmoil in the Middle East. A little impatience led to a lot of trouble.

God does not work when we demand him to; he works when he is ready to. Faith responds to God and resists the urge to do what he wants done before he wants it done. Some of us need to stop giving God deadlines. It is not a good idea to get in the habit of telling God when he needs to do something. While it is true that he places in us and before us the things we need to trust him for, we must keep in mind that he doesn't work for us. We work for him. We move when he says move and we wait when he says wait. Again, both require faith.

Waiting causes us to appreciate and savor God's sovereign control over our lives. As we place our anxieties in his hands and release control of our lives completely to his loving care, our faith is rewarded with sustaining grace and power. We think we will break because we have to wait. Instead, God meets us and stretches us. As we will see shortly, the process of waiting for God to provide has a way of shifting our attachment from that which we are trusting him for to the Giver of the gift and the Fulfiller of the promise, God himself. If he gives us what we are trusting him for too soon, we may become more attached to the provision than to the Provider. God will not allow us to worship what he gives to us. He does not want us to worship what we long for, but to worship the Giver of our longings, God alone.

### The Unclear Reason

That introduces the third point that Abraham teaches us: *to obey when we don't know why God is asking us to do the excruciating.*

Can we sacrifice the very thing God promised to us? That's the question that grabs us from Hebrews 11:17–19. Look again at those words: "By faith Abraham, when he was tested, offered up Isaac, and he who had received the promises was in the act of offering up his only son, of whom it was said, 'Through Isaac shall your offspring be named.' He considered that God was able even to raise him from the dead, from which, figuratively speaking, he did receive him back."

This passage is a summary of Genesis 22:1–14. Think about it: God told Abraham, "Take your son, your only son Isaac, whom you love, and go to the land of Moriah, and offer him there as a burnt offering on one of the mountains of which I shall tell you" (v. 2). Wait a minute! Isaac was the miracle baby. He was the only son of Abraham and Sarah. He was the son of the promise. God had promised that the world would be blessed through him. Surely God did not literally mean for Abraham to slay his son.

How did Abraham respond? In the very next verse we read, "So Abraham rose early in the morning, saddled his donkey, and took two of his young men with him, and his son Isaac. And he cut the wood for the burnt offering and arose and went to the place of which God had told him" (v. 3). The depth and immediacy of Abraham's obedience takes my breath away. God gave him a clear directive. Abraham didn't deliberate. He didn't question God. He didn't try to solve his dilemma. He did one thing. He obeyed.

By this point in Abraham's walk with God, he had learned that faith is obedience—even if that obedience threatens the very thing you have longed for, loved, and cherished. Once again, faith focuses on God and not on that for which we are trusting him. God gives us desires and promises not so that we grow attached to the fulfillment and realization, but so that our hearts are more fully and completely devoted to the God of the promise. If we cannot give back to God that which he has given to us, then what he has given to us has taken the place of God.

This is a sad but all-too-common trap. It's like the pastor who has a dream to plant a church. There are little or no resources, just a vision on his heart from the Lord. He takes obedient, sacrificial steps of faith, and God blesses and honors him. People come to Christ and the church grows. Soon there are multiple services over the weekend, and the pastor has become an admired, respected, and sought-after leader. But his sense of identity, value, and significance is now tied to what God has done. Ironically, he has a very difficult time placing what has been accomplished back into the hands of the One who did it all. It's his "baby," and he won't place it on the altar.

Remember, whatever God gives to us is to be placed back into his hands. Is there something that you will not give up in order to obey God? Career? Reputation? Success? Family? If we cannot sacrifice it, God does not own it. We have stalled on our faith journey.

## LESSONS ON FAITH AND SACRIFICE

This supreme test of Abraham's faith teaches us that obedient faith will make us do extraordinarily difficult things. But it also teaches us some precious, priceless lessons concerning the relationship between faith and sacrifice. I hope these observations will pour hope and encouragement into your soul.

First, as we have seen, it is one thing to trust God while we are waiting for something, but it is quite another thing to trust and obey him after we receive it. It becomes our source of security, and fear of losing the "gift" weakens and diminishes our faith. We justify our vanishing faith with sanitized expressions, such as, "I paid my dues." The greater challenge to our faith is how we view God's provision after we receive it.

Second, while the tests of faith may become more difficult as we walk with God, the rewards are more wonderful. As Abraham raised his hand to slay his son, God stopped him and pointed to the ram caught in the thicket (Gen. 22:11–14). This was God's "last-minute" provision to replace Isaac. I doubt very seriously that Abraham ever again questioned God's ability to provide. Likewise, the more we trust God, the sweeter we find his provision.

Third, there are tests of faith that defy logic and that we want to resist. The truth of the matter is that from time to time, God calls us to trust him for things and to do things that don't make a lot of sense. It is a dangerous thing to live the Christian life assuming that God will never lead us to do anything that is not logical or reasonable.

I became a pastor at age fifty-five, and trust me, that did not make a whole lot of sense. There were a lot more reasonable, easier things I could have done. But I would have missed out on the miracles, joy, and fruit God had waiting for me. Please, don't allow your assumptions and the need for a predictable life to drain the supernatural out of your walk with God.

Fourth, true faith holds nothing back from God. Nothing. Genesis 22 teaches us that our families should not be idols. Although I am thrilled with today's emphasis among evangelicals on making our homes and families a priority, I must confess that I am a bit concerned that some Christians have slipped into idolatry. When the desired comfort of our families trumps obedience to God's leading or when we seldom make justifiable sacrifices for service opportunities, we may have made the family our default God. Everything belongs on the altar.

Finally, sacrificial faith is liberating. When we release back to God what he has given to us, we disentangle ourselves from this world and affirm our complete, sole allegiance to him. Not only does our faith grow, but our courage grows as well. We live, act, and respond before an audience of one. No longer conflicted, we stare down our fears and we keep trusting God in the dark, lonely places. The freedom comes when God removes every other source of security and we realize that he is all we have—and all we need.

God gets us to this point when, as he did with Abraham, he calls us to take steps of obedient faith when we don't know exactly where we are going, when we don't know when he will fulfill his promise, and when we don't know why he is calling us to do the excruciating. We follow because we trust him.

## QUESTIONS FOR DISCUSSION OR REFLECTION

1. Is there an area of your life in which you struggle to "live by faith"? In what areas of your life do you find it easy to live by faith?

2. When have you had to take a step forward in faith before you had the resources you "needed"? How did that experience turn out?

3. Second Peter 3:9 tells us, "The Lord is not slow to fulfill his promise, as some count slowness, but is patient toward you, not wishing that any should perish, but that all should reach repentance." When has the Lord's "slowness" been for your good?

4. Sometimes waiting shows lack of faith. Sometimes impatience shows a lack of faith. How can we move forward in wisdom, keeping pace with the Holy Spirit?

# 5

# Faith Is Destiny

I am a child of the great migration. From the early 1900s until about 1970, millions of African-Americans left the South and flooded such cities as New York, Philadelphia, Detroit, Chicago, and Los Angeles. They were tired of the oppressive segregation in the South and were looking for jobs that would provide more opportunity for their families. In 1942, Crawford and Sylvia Loritts (my parents) moved from North Carolina to Newark, New Jersey. My two older sisters and I were born there.

Our parents, like so many other African-Americans of their generation, raised us with a sense of obligation and gratitude for those who came before us and who were denied the opportunities and freedoms that we had. We were expected to be good stewards of what had been placed in our hands. This would be our tribute to those who had sacrificed on our behalf and deferred their dreams and hopes to a time that they would never see, but one that their children and grandchildren might experience. In this regard, they paid our tuition and expected a return on their investment.

So when I or my sisters seemed to be getting sidetracked or to be heading down a path that had irresponsibility written all over it, Pop would give us "the speech." He had various versions of the speech, depending on how far off course he thought we were. But in short, it went something like this: "Do you know and appreciate what you have and the opportunities before you? Let me remind you of what your uncles and aunts had to go through, not to mention your grandfather and your great-grandfather Peter (the former slave). And by the way, do you know why I'm working so hard? That's right: so that you can do better than we could have done. Now step up and act like you're going somewhere."

My father was not a legalistic tyrant. He just understood heritage and legacy. He knew that if we appreciated and valued where we had come from and kept our sights on where we were going, we would stay focused. Others had walked the path before us. They had had more obstacles in their way than we did. They had paid a dear price, but they had kept moving. Why? Hope. Although they did not experience the fulfillment of their dreams, they anticipated something better for the next generation, and they believed that when they stepped into God's presence, he would reward them. Their love, commitment, and perseverance were both our encouragement and our stewardship. They were fuel for our faith.

This idea of looking to the future is the focus of Hebrews 11:13–16:

> These all died in faith, not having received the things promised, but having seen them and greeted them from afar, and having acknowledged that they were strangers and exiles on the earth. For people who speak thus make it clear that they are seeking a homeland. If they had been thinking of that land from which they had gone out, they would have had opportunity to return. But as it is, they desire a better coun-

try, that is, a heavenly one. Therefore God is not ashamed to be called their God, for he has prepared for them a city.

In this section, the writer of Hebrews speaks of faith as a noble journey toward a destiny. The journey is not conditioned by time or our moment in history. God places on our hearts some things that we are to trust him for, and even if we do not experience them in our lifetimes, our hope for them provides fuel for the journey. In other words, we have a vision of what could be; what should be; what *ought* to be. The vision is so important, so right, that it demands that we give ourselves completely to it.

This kind of vision was what kept so many in the civil-rights movement pressing forward. The time had come. Freedom and equality were almost within their reach. This is what Martin Luther King Jr. was referring to when he uttered those eerily prophetic words at a rally at a church in Memphis: "I've been to the mountaintop. . . . I've seen the Promised Land. I may not get there with you. But . . . we, as a people, will get to the Promised Land."[6] The very next day, April 4, 1968, he was shot and killed.

Those who died in the civil-rights struggle did not die in vain. What they believed should happen and would happen was worth giving their lives to, even if they did not experience in their lifetimes the reward of their struggle. Their courage and sacrifice have inspired those of us who have followed them to press forward.

This is legacy faith. It is a faith that is resilient and timeless. It is not a faith that we express, but a faith that characterizes us. We *are* people of faith. Faith becomes both our motivation and our identity. In other words, we are the people who believe God. That faith, that holy confidence, has kept previous generations moving, and it has been handed off to us to accomplish the same end.

## TRUE FREEDOM

What did this legacy-building, identity-forming faith produce in these noble pilgrims described in Hebrews 11:13–16?

It made them *free*.

At first glance, the opening line of verse 13 seems to suggest that their faith let them down. God didn't come through. Look at the words: "These all died in faith, not having received the things promised." There you have it. God promised it. They believed it. But they never received it. They died. But look again. Notice that they "all died *in* faith." What's the point? Their faith had not diminished, even though in their lifetimes they could not wrap their arms around the promises they were trusting God to fulfill. They were not reduced to cynicism and unbelief. To the contrary, their faith was strong when they died. Remember, they all died "in faith."

So their faith was not defined by the *what*. No, I'm not playing word games here. God does what he promises. But sometimes what he promises can become the object of our faith, an idol. When what we want—even what God promised to us—becomes the focus of our affections and an object of worship, we have walked right into bondage. We have placed God on trial, and when he does not come through when we want him to, we judge that he is not worthy of our faith because, in our minds, he cannot be trusted.

Does this mean that we hedge our bets by not "getting our hopes too high"? No, as we have seen through the example of Abraham, we keep pressing forward in faith even when we don't know when or how God is going to bring it all together.

And what will others think when our faith is not made visible and fulfilled? We obey to express our faith, not to impress others or look good in their eyes. Sometimes obeying God makes us look foolish. God uses faith to set us free of our pride and people pleasing.

The price that faith pays is self-denial. Wasn't that the message to Gideon (Judges 6–8)? God told Gideon that he was going to defeat the mighty Midianite army. However, Gideon's set of assumptions didn't line up with God's plan. God reduced Gideon's resources to a pitiful fraction of what he felt he needed to be victorious. Gideon was faced with a seemingly impossible situation. Defeat looked certain. If Gideon survived, he would face a life sentence of embarrassment and shame. But Gideon pressed forward in faith. Why? Because God had brought him to the place where he understood that his faith was defined by and anchored in the *who*—God—and not the *what*. It didn't matter what others thought. He had nothing to prove. He was free.

This is true freedom. When we are "reduced" to looking to God alone, we are free of all other distractions and the need to perform for audiences that quite frankly don't matter. When our resources are dried up and all we have is God, we are free from the temptation of idolatry, because all of the idols are gone. When we are one on one with God, we learn and embrace what one sage said: "When all you have is God, you realize that he is all you need." You see, faith's lesson is not about getting from God what we want, but discovering and experiencing the sufficiency of God in all things. It is always, only about God. God certainly does what he promises, but he does so in order that he will be glorified in every situation and challenge in life. Knowing this brings holy relief and freedom.

## A REAL FUTURE

Because we are free to look to God alone, we can live in the reality of the future. The next line of Hebrews 11:13 says, "but having seen [the things promised] and greeted them from afar . . ." This is astonishing. These great pilgrims did not treat what God had promised them as if it were an abstract idea or a mythical representation of what they understood to be God's message to them or what *could* happen. Neither did they, in the name of common sense and reason, park their forward movement to see if it all would really happen. This very statement implies that they refused to be restrained or inhibited by doubt and unbelief. In short, they knew that if God had said it, then it was a reality—even if they had not yet experienced it.

It's like the story of the elderly lady who lived in a town that was experiencing a severe drought. But she believed in her heart that the Lord had impressed upon her that rain was coming soon. So on a hot and very dry evening, she showed up at church with her umbrella, raincoat, and galoshes. When she was asked why she had all that rain gear, she said, "Because I'm expecting it to rain!"

Faith is not speculation. Remember, Hebrews 11:1 says, "Now faith is the *assurance* of things hoped for, the *conviction* of things not seen." Faith lives in the reality of what it believes. It views the future as if it were real. This is not to say that people who are filled with faith cannot function in the "now" and are out of touch with reality. It means that their behavior and actions reflect confidence in God, in what he has promised, and in what he has placed in their hearts to trust him for. As my dad would sometimes say to me when my behavior did not match my goals, "Son, you're going somewhere, so act like it!"

Further, we learn from these great men and women of God

that we should embrace and cherish the vision, the fulfillment of that for which we are trusting God. Verse 13 says that they "greeted [the things promised] from afar." The word *greet* means "to salute or welcome." This is not to be taken in the sense of a casual handshake or a pat on the back when we run into someone we know. It's more like a joyful reunion with a dear friend or loved one we have not seen for a while. For example, all of us are moved when we see videos of the reunions of military moms and dads with their families after long tours of duty overseas. There are tears of joy as a deep longing is fulfilled. In the same way, we wrap our arms around the vision and the dreams God has placed in our hearts.

My parents are with the Lord. They were ordinary people who lived life with hope and anticipation. There wasn't a hint of bitterness in them concerning the opportunities that were denied them and their generation. I guess they were too busy raising three children and placing in our hearts and hands what they could taste, what they knew would happen. They refused to live in discouragement or allow anybody to define what a Loritts could or could not be. In that sense, they greeted the vision from afar and embraced it as a reality. I guess you could say that what they saw became a dear friend and an ally that moved them along their journey.

What things has God placed in your heart that should mark your moment in history? Treat them as dear friends and greet them as realities. Embrace them as tools in God's hands to shape you. See them as his mighty channels of blessing and spiritual impact on the lives of those with whom you come in contact. Don't be discouraged by the gap between where you are and what you see. In fact, if there is no gap, then the vision is not of faith, and God has no opportunity to prove his sufficiency in and through your life. Treat the vision as the reality, and our mighty God will bridge the gap.

## A GLORIOUS DESTINATION

Hebrews 11:13 also teaches us that as long as we are in this world, we are always out of place: "and having acknowledged that they were strangers and exiles on the earth . . ." Like these pilgrims, we too are to accept and acknowledge what is true about every follower of Christ—this world is not our home.

In recent years, the evangelical approach to the Christian life, perhaps unintentionally, has tended to downplay the motivation of our home, our destination: heaven. We want a Christianity that "works" and that is attractive. We want to give people transferable, practical ways to resolve conflict, raise nice kids, solve the communication problems in their marriages, and be smart money managers. We don't want to be viewed as weird, so we lead with the pragmatic stuff of the Christian life. After all, why talk about stuff that people are not interested in and that won't address their immediate felt needs?

Don't get me wrong. I'm in favor of being practical and help-ful. The Word of God speaks to every issue and circumstance in life, and we should search the Scriptures and apply what they say to whatever need we have. But we do this not because we want to be "cool" Christians and court the approval and endorsement of the world. We do these things not to prove to the world that we are an improved, attractive brand of the prevailing world system. Christianity is not about improvement but about transformation. It is not about replacing stuff that doesn't "work" with stuff that does. It is about redeeming lost people and living as those who have been given the gift of eternal life, as those who live for and are motivated by their eternal destination.

Followers of Christ are strangers and exiles in this world. In short, we don't belong here. What makes the difference is that we are different. We live as if we're not tethered to this life. We are from another world, one that operates by different, distinct values—enduring, eternal values. And because we realize that we carry with us that which every person was born to experience, we give the world what it desperately needs instead of trying to be a renovated version of a condemned house.

We were born for God's presence and we keep moving toward his presence. C. S. Lewis said it best: "If I discover within myself a desire which no experience in this world can satisfy, the most probable explanation is that I was made for another world."[7] We are visitors in a foreign country ("strangers"). We're not permanent residents. We are here to model the destination. We travel light. We are free, fluid, and flexible. The Word of God fills our tanks, and faith-filled steps of obedience keep us moving through this land. In turn, we become noble, compelling portraits of what eternal life is and what all of us can be.

Faith presupposes that we are going somewhere and that God is doing something in and through us. During our journey through this life, he gives us assignments, challenges, and a vision that can be met and fulfilled only through faith. Keep in mind that others are watching as our great God works for us and through us. As he works, God demonstrates his sufficiency and is glorified. In turn, many are drawn to the God of the people from another world. Our faith and obedience unlock their hunger and longing for God and home.

## A LASER FOCUS

Faith that is characterized by this kind of freedom is *focused*. It has made up its mind. We see this in verses 14 and 15: "For people who speak thus make it clear that they are seeking a homeland. If they had been thinking of that land from which they had gone out, they would have had opportunity to return."

There are two crucial truths in these verses.

First, *here* is not what we are looking for. We are "seeking a homeland." The eighteenth-century evangelist John Wesley was invited by a plantation owner to tour his vast estate. They rode their horses for hours and saw only a fraction of the man's property. At the end of the day, they sat down for dinner, and the plantation owner eagerly asked, "Well, Mr. Wesley, what do you think?" Wesley replied, "I think you are going to have a hard time leaving all of this."[8] As followers of Christ, we should enjoy life, but we shouldn't be attached to it. Faith keeps us walking toward home.

Second, *there* is not worth going back to. Verse 15 says that these faith-filled pilgrims did not have a replay button. Once they were clear about the call of God, where he wanted them to go and what he wanted them to trust him for, they headed off in that direction. They chose not to go back. They knew that where God was taking them was better than where they came from.

That's not to say that they weren't tempted to make a U-turn. During those trying moments in the wilderness, I suppose Moses thought, "Working for my father-in-law was a piece of cake compared to putting up with the rebellious nonsense of two million people." But returning was not an option. Faith-filled obedience pleases God, so Moses drew his strength from God and kept moving forward.

How do you think David felt? (Actually, he tells us in the Psalms.) He never asked to be king. He didn't campaign for the position. It was God's assignment for him. Soon, however, King Saul's jealousy morphed into insanity. So for the next sixteen years, David was running for his life. Can't you just hear David saying: "Man, you know what? Who needs this hiding out in caves and all of these crazy folks trying to kill me? Why didn't I just drop off the lunch to my brothers, leave Goliath alone, and go on back to watching Daddy's sheep?" But he didn't go back. Like Moses, David drew his strength from God and kept moving forward.

Destiny-shaping faith is not ambivalent and conflicted, trying to embrace and justify competing values and directions. Once God makes clear what it is we must trust him for and pursue, we head in that direction. Our faith-filled obedience says that nothing is more important than his voice and his plan for our lives.

## A BETTER COUNTRY

Verse 16 tells us that these faith-filled pilgrims were driven by a vision of a fulfilled future: "They desire a better country, that is, a heavenly one. Therefore God is not ashamed to be called their God."

They knew that the ultimate payoff for their faith-filled obedience was not in this life, but in the very presence of God. In fact, what God placed on their hearts to believe him for stirred the passion in their hearts for heaven ("they desire a better country").

When we exercise faith, we cultivate an appetite for the future. When we refuse to settle for a "comfortable complacency," we step into the adventure of our lives. We learn that what God places on our hearts to believe him for is always better than what we are tempted to settle for. We begin to press forward with anticipation. What more does God have in store? We experience his supernatural intervention and provision, whetting our appetites for that city "whose designer and builder is God" (v. 10).

Like these pilgrims, our hearts embrace the reality that all of the beauty and appeal of this world is inferior to where we are going.

This faith-filled obedience moves God's heart. He is proud to be associated with us. Look at the second part of verse 16: "Therefore, God is not ashamed to be called their God." Not only is God not embarrassed by us, but he wants to put us on display. We have drawn his holy attention and favor. He empowers us and tells his story through our lives, all because we have chosen the path of faith and obedience. We become his living, breathing object lessons of what he can do through those who trust him. The more we trust him, the more we experience him. The more we experience him, the more others see him. All of this happens because we stepped away from a theoretical Christianity and said to God: "I will take you at your word and I will keep moving toward what you have placed on my heart to trust you for. By your grace and strength, I won't go back."

## QUESTIONS FOR DISCUSSION OR REFLECTION

1. Why is a vision of what *ought to be* essential for helping us act with faith in the present?

2. When have you placed more hope in your dream than in God, who gave you the dream? When have you released a dream to follow a new direction from God?

3. In 2 Samuel 7, King David expresses his desire to build a temple for God. God has different plans. Read 2 Samuel 7.

4. In Jeremiah 32, Jeremiah is so confident God will return his people to their homeland that Jeremiah buys a field in Jerusalem. Is God asking you to take a step of faith? What is it?

# 6

# Faith Is Mission

As followers of Christ, we are described as God's "workmanship, created in Christ Jesus for good works, which God prepared beforehand, that *we should walk in them*" (Eph. 2:10). God has a plan for us. Our job is to find out what it is ("good works"), live it out, experience it, and express it ("walk in them"). That requires faith.

To be sure, sometimes the "good works" are right in front of us and there is little if any opposition. We're not inconvenienced in doing them. We have the resources we need. Doing them doesn't cost us anything and brings us great joy. In such instances, not much faith is required. But some assignments are above our "pay grade," beyond our capacity and capabilities, inconvenient, and full of barriers and opposition. Yet we know that they are what God has for us. To retreat would be disobedience. In these instances, faith is our *only* option.

Faith is all about overcoming and pressing through opposition. Why? It's clear and simple: God wants to be glorified in and through our lives, and the greater the opposition, the greater the glory—his glory. This is a dominant theme of the Bible. In fact, as you read the Scriptures, you can identify what can be called a sacred pattern:

1. Vision: God makes clear to us what he wants us to do or to believe him for.
2. Opposition: The vision is threatened. It becomes increasingly difficult, if not impossible, to fulfill and achieve. We're at the Red Sea. We're about to be thrown into the "fiery furnace." Our ship is sinking.
3. Intervention: When all the doors seem to be closed and locked, and it seems as if there is nothing we can do, God steps in. He delivers us. He meets the need. He solves the problem and resolves the dilemma. He does it, not we.
4. Celebration: God uses his intervention as an object lesson about his greatness and glory. We put the spotlight on God and stand back in awe and wonder. He alone did it.
5. Transformation: We are changed and marked by the power and presence of our great God. Our faith is strengthened and we are encouraged to trust him for more.

But how we handle the opposition tells the story. We need to seriously consider what we are missing when we allow opposition to stop us and turn us back. Think about it: we won't know God's intervention and deliverance because we have "delivered" ourselves by turning back. There won't be depth and richness in our worship because we will have very little personal experience and few stories of God delivering us. Like muscles that are not used, our faith will atrophy because we refused to exercise it. We will mainstream fear and, in so doing, disinvite God's supernatural presence. We will have missed God's moment.

There will always be opposition from any number of places. Remember, we don't live the Christian life in a neutral environment; we have an enemy. There is a war going on between the kingdom of darkness and the kingdom of light, and as followers of Christ (citizens of the kingdom of light), we are on the front lines, engaged in the battle. Of course, the Devil does not want us to fulfill God's plans for our lives, so he's not going to leave us alone. Let's not be naive. He will throw at us whatever he can to discourage us and stop us. But we can press forward, protected by the shield of faith (Eph. 6:16).

Faith is called "faith" *because it confronts that which stands in the way of God's plan and assignments for our lives.* So, once again, faith is not only our response to the challenges we face, but also movement toward the fulfillment of God's plan for us.

In this chapter, I want to take a closer look at some of the things that stand in the way, threatening and impeding our steps of obedience toward fully realizing the mission we were born to accomplish and experience—those "good works."

For our encouragement and motivation, in Hebrews 11:23–31, we have accounts of how Moses, Joshua, and Rahab kept moving toward the fulfillment of God's assignments for them despite the opposition and roadblocks in their way:

> By faith Moses, when he was born, was hidden for three months by his parents, because they saw that the child was beautiful, and they were not afraid of the king's edict. By faith Moses, when he was grown up, refused to be called the son of Pharaoh's daughter, choosing rather to be mistreated with the people of God than to enjoy the fleeting pleasures of sin. He considered the reproach of Christ greater wealth than the treasures of Egypt, for he was looking to the reward. By faith he left Egypt, not being afraid of the anger of the king, for he endured as seeing him who is invisible. By faith he kept the Passover and sprinkled the blood, so that the Destroyer of the firstborn might not touch them.
>
> By faith the people crossed the Red Sea as on dry land, but the Egyptians, when they attempted to do the same, were drowned. By faith the walls of Jericho fell down after they had been encircled for seven days. By faith Rahab the

prostitute did not perish with those who were disobedient, because she had given a friendly welcome to the spies.

In this passage, we find seven roadblocks to their mission and their faith that Moses, Joshua, and Rahab faced. Centuries separate us, but our roadblocks and opposition are the same.

## THE ROADBLOCK OF THE FUTURE

We are often intimidated about the future. The odds are against us. Charting our progress through our circumstances, we see that we're not trending upward. It just doesn't make sense to move forward. We are tempted to accept the painful reality, bury the dream, grieve the loss, create a "new normal," and deal with what we can see and control.

Moses's parents had every reason to embrace this attitude. But they didn't. Look at Hebrews 11:23: "By faith Moses, when he was born, was hidden for three months by his parents, because they saw that the child was beautiful, and they were not afraid of the king's edict."

This verse is a summary of the events outlined in Exodus 1:6–2:10. Joseph, the son of Jacob, was loved by Pharaoh and was made second in command in Egypt. Jacob's family moved to Egypt, where they prospered. In fact, Exodus 1:7 says, "But the people of Israel were fruitful and increased greatly; they multiplied and grew exceedingly strong, so that the land was filled with them." Then things began to change. A new king (Pharaoh), who hadn't known Joseph, came to power. He was more than intimidated by the prosperity of the Jews and the explosive growth in their population. His solution was vicious, oppressive enslavement of them (vv. 8–14). Further, he instructed the Jewish midwives to kill any boy that was born (vv. 15–16). But the midwives wouldn't do this because they feared God (v. 17).

Pharaoh then told all Egyptian people that if they found a Jewish baby boy, they were to throw him into the Nile River (v. 22), where he would drown or be eaten by crocodiles.

Enter Moses's parents. They didn't believe that God wanted their son killed. They believed that God had something more, something better for their future and the future of their baby boy. Through the eyes of faith, they stared down the future (Heb. 11:23). This faith caused them to come up with a plan. It was God's plan. They put the baby in a basket in a strategic, safe place in the Nile River where they knew members of the Egyptian royal family would be bathing. All the while, their daughter, Moses's sister, was watching, hidden behind the brush. Pharaoh's daughter "discovered" the basket with baby Moses inside. Moses's mother became his nurse, and Pharaoh's daughter raised Moses as her son (Ex. 2:1–10).

Think about it: Why did Moses's parents choose faith-filled, courageous action? Certainly they could have concluded: "Who are we compared to these mighty Egyptians? Look at us! We're slaves, and everything about us is controlled by the Egyptians, including our future. There's no way we can save our son's life. We ought to thank God for the weeks we've had with him and take joy and consolation in the daughter that we have."

But they fought this mindset. Why? Granted, every parent will fight to the death to save his or her children. But there is something more here. Hebrews 11:23 says, "They were not afraid of the king's edict." To be sure, Pharaoh was an extraordinarily powerful man who believed that he held life and death in his hands. Why, then, weren't Moses's parents afraid of the edict, the command, of Pharaoh? The answer is seen in their faith-filled action. They believed that God and God alone controls the future, so they acted accordingly. Although Pharaoh acted as if he was in charge, they knew that the Ancient of Days, the God of Abraham, Isaac, and Jacob, has the last word. He is the God of today and tomorrow.

Their response also teaches us that faith does not acquiesce. It doesn't fold under the pressure and uncertainty of the future. As we have seen, faith presupposes not only opposition, but a fight. In this case, faith refused to accept the conventional wisdom that baby Moses would die. His parents weren't going to give up until God said so. They fought doubt and unbelief, and in so doing, they declared the power and sufficiency of God in all things.

What about you? Does the future pose a threat to what God has placed on your heart to trust him for? Have you backed away from faith because you just can't figure out how it all can happen? Have you rationalized and repackaged your fear of the future to make it appear to yourself and others that you are "prudent," "wise," and "spiritual"?

## THE ROADBLOCK OF COMFORT

Although Moses was raised as the son of Pharaoh's daughter, his future was not to be that of a privileged Egyptian. Hebrews 11:24–26 says: "By faith Moses, when he was grown up, refused to be called the son of Pharaoh's daughter, choosing rather to be mistreated with the people of God than to enjoy the fleeting pleasures of sin. He considered the reproach of Christ greater wealth than the treasures of Egypt, for he was looking to the reward."

We express our faith by our obedience to God's call and plan for our lives. Faith clings tightly to God and his Word, but holds everything else with an open hand. Therefore, faith is willing to sacrifice whatever it takes to pursue and fulfill God's will.

That's the point of the expression in verse 26, which says that Moses "considered the reproach of Christ greater wealth than the treasures of Egypt." Moses's choice to identify with God's people foreshadowed their deliverance and pointed to the ultimate deliverer, Jesus Christ.

Moses was all in. He relinquished all entitlement to a life of privilege and comfort in exchange for the joy of faith-filled obedience to God. If necessary, faith chooses the deeper pleasure of disgrace for Christ's sake over the temporary, superficial pleasures of a comfortable life. Indeed, it is better to be disgraced in the eyes of the world than to be seduced into a comfortable, pleasurable disobedience.

We need to take a serious look at our assumptions. Most of us in the West, especially in the United States, assume that God's plan for our lives includes increasing prosperity. We take for granted that we will make more money, get bigger houses, buy more clothes, accumulate more stuff—and the list goes on. No, I'm not suggesting that wealth is evil and that capping our lifestyle will make us more godly. (I know quite a few godly, generous, faith-filled followers of Christ who happen to be wealthy.) The question is not how much we have, but what we value. In other words, what—or more appropriately, who—do we treasure above and beyond everything that we have? Do we love God more than we love our lifestyle? If God were to make clear that his next assignment for you would involve significantly downsizing your material appetites and what you've grown accustomed to having, would you do it? In obedience to Christ, can you walk away from what you have accumulated?

I have a young friend who is a pediatric surgeon. He is good at what he does and has enjoyed a very comfortable life, with the promise of even greater financial rewards. He and his dear wife are committed followers of Christ. A few years ago, God began tugging on their hearts concerning the need for medical care for children in a country in West Africa. It became clear that God was calling them to meet this need. In obedience, they left the comfort of their careers in the United States, and they are now serving as medical missionaries in West Africa. And, I might add, their hearts are filled with joy.

Faith means sacrifice, including humiliation in the eyes of others. Moses considered the "reproach" associated with his obedience to God of greater value than the treasures of Egypt. In essence, he was saying, "I will gladly give up their approval to know and experience what they scorn but desperately need, the approval and pleasure of God."

Comfort and privilege are poor substitutes for the soul-enriching joy that comes from a faith that is free and unencumbered.

## THE ROADBLOCK OF SECURITY

Hebrews 11:27 says, "By faith [Moses] left Egypt, not being afraid of the anger of the king, for he endured as seeing him who is invisible." If you are familiar with the story of Moses, this verse may pose a bit of a problem. You might be thinking: "Wait a minute! According to Exodus 2:11–15, Moses killed an Egyptian he saw beating a Hebrew, the word got out, and he left Egypt because he was afraid when he heard that Pharaoh wanted to kill him for what he had done."

Yes, Moses left Egypt the *first* time because he was afraid. But I believe that Hebrews 11:27 is referring to the exodus. After Moses encountered God at the burning bush and God made clear what his assignment was, fear of Pharaoh, or of any human being for that matter, was taken off the table. Under

God's direct orders, Moses went back to Egypt, walked into the palace, looked Pharaoh in the eye, and said, "God says, 'Let my people go.'"

Moses had met with God, and God had become his source of strength and security (Ex. 3:1–4:17). Please don't miss this. During the forty years Moses had spent in exile after leaving Egypt the first time, God had stripped him of the security and stability that his place and prominence in Egypt had afforded him. He had been reduced to working as a shepherd, an occupation despised by the proud Egyptians. As the adopted grandson of Pharaoh, he had been set for life; his options for the future were virtually limitless. By leaving, he had forfeited riches and the security of a stable future. Finally, Moses had nothing to prove, and God said, in essence, "You're now ready for me to use you." When Moses encountered God through the burning bush, everything changed. God marked him and anchored him for the rest of his life. Thereafter, Moses took courageous steps of faith because he knew that God was his identity and security.

From this point on in Moses's life, God parsed out his plan in pieces, telling Moses just enough for him to know what to do next. This was to keep Moses and the people dependent on God. God wanted them and the generations that followed to know that he alone was their security.

Faith is a risky business because it focuses on God alone as our security. But then again, that's no risk. As he did with Moses, God sometimes takes everything away from us except himself. Then, when we are forced to fix our undistracted gaze on him, we're struck with the awe-inspiring realization that he's more than we've ever needed. You see, sometimes too many options, opportunities, and provisions set us up for smug self-reliance and idolatry. We may say that we are walking by faith, but our real security is found in our resources, relationships, and place in life. Of course, we never speak the words, but our attitudes and actions say that if God doesn't come through, we have a backup plan. The reality is that if God were to back away from us, there isn't a backup plan in the world that could save our necks.

Faith makes the decision that it will never use God's gifts to replace God. Put another way, the provision is not the Provider. Our arms are wrapped tightly around God, not around our plans for the future and the stuff that we think will get us "there." We are most free and useful to God when we come to the place where we truly believe that he is enough.

Faith is our response to God's call to transfer our sense of security from everything else to him. If we fail to make the transfer, then God's holy "what could have been through you" will never be fully realized. When it comes to trusting anything other than God, giving up means going forward. Is there anything that you're holding onto that's holding you back from fully trusting God for your future and the assignments that he has for you?

## THE ROADBLOCK OF DISOBEDIENCE

Hebrews 11:28 says, "By faith [Moses] kept the Passover and sprinkled the blood, so that the Destroyer of the firstborn might not touch them."

Moses did what God told him to do. As the opening line of verse 28 says, "By faith he *kept* the Passover." If you read the account of the Passover in Exodus 12, you realize that Moses did not vary from what God told him to do. He didn't interpret it. He didn't change it to fit what he might have wanted God to do. Think about it: this final plague on the Egyptians was horrific. Pharaoh's stubborn disobedience had mocked God, and God had had enough. He sent the death angel to kill all of the firstborn. The Jewish families could escape this terror only by sprinkling the blood of lambs on their doorframes. This was literally a matter of life and death. It was not the time to fudge on the details. And Moses didn't. He did what God told him to do.

As we saw in a previous chapter, faith and obedience are two sides of the same coin. There is no faith apart from obedience, and obedience requires faith. Once God makes clear what the assignment is, what he wants done, and/or how he wants it done, he expects obedient action. As we have seen, sometimes God gives us the details of what he wants us to do and to trust him for. At other times, he gives us just enough information to take the next step. In either case, God expects us to obey him, to do what he is clearly leading us to do.

Faith flourishes when we press through and fight our natural inclination to disobey God. We are sinful, self-centered creatures who love being in control and expect God to relate to us on our terms. We want to wait until it is "comfortable" and convenient to obey God. We want to be ready to obey him. But more often than not, it's the other way around. First we obey, then God makes us ready.

Are you hesitant to respond to God's next assignment for you because you just don't want to do what you know in your heart is God's clear direction for you? For about two years before my wife, Karen, and I left the staff of Cru, I knew that God was leading me to be a pastor. But I resisted. One day, Karen turned to me and said, "Honey, when are you going to pay attention to this?" She knew that there was a bit of a struggle going on inside of me. The Holy Spirit used her question to send me a warning—if I didn't pursue what God had placed on my heart to do, there would be consequences. I had to be obedient to his leading and take steps of faith as he pointed me toward where he wanted me to be.

## THE ROADBLOCK OF DREAD

Finally, Pharaoh had had enough, or so it seemed. He told Moses to take the more than two million Jews and go (Ex. 12:31–32). They gathered their belongings and headed off with Moses toward the Promised Land, leaving slavery and oppression behind. Oh, the joy and promise of a new beginning and a bright future! They were finally free. They had no reason to think that there would be any serious, life-threatening opposition in their way.

Their optimism was quickly erased. Pharaoh changed his mind, gathered his army, and came after the Jews (Ex. 14:5–8). Because of the route God led them on, Moses and the people were stuck—the Red Sea was in front of them and the mighty Egyptian army was within sight (v. 9). In the people's minds, the question was not whether they were going to die but how: "Do we march forward and drown in the Red Sea or do we stay here and get butchered by the army?" Forgetting the miracles they had seen God perform (the ten plagues), the people panicked and turned on Moses. They were seized by the darkest form of fear, a paralyzing dread that encased them in a sense of doom. So they said to Moses, "Is it because there are no graves in Egypt that you have taken us away to die in the wilderness?" (v. 11).

How did Moses respond? What did he say? No, he didn't cave in and say: "I know. We have come to the end of the line. Let's just pray that it will be over quickly." He faced the people and the crisis with the steely resolve of faith. Verse 13 sends chills down my spine. Moses said, "Fear not, stand firm, and see the salvation of the Lord, which he will work for you today." Moses believed God's promise in the darkest hour, and he told the people to do the same.

God's promises are not canceled out by our crises. Absolutely nothing stands in the way of God's accomplishing and fulfilling what he says he will do.

Miracles are a part of the plan. God said to Moses: "Tell the people of Israel to go forward. Lift up your staff, and stretch out your hand over the sea and divide it, that the people of Israel may go through the sea on dry ground" (vv. 15–16). God told the people to march toward the Red Sea, the very thing that they were afraid would kill them. Faith confronts and challenges our worst fears. As I said earlier, we will never know God's intervention until we face what can undo and destroy us. Sooner or later, we have to have a showdown with what we fear. Our faith is only as strong as what we are willing to face.

The people moved forward. They crossed the Red Sea on dry land. Not even their feet got wet. However, the Egyptian army drowned. And God did all of this to underscore his greatness in the eyes of his people. He wanted them to know, and for there to be a permanent, eternal record, that he never fails. Truly faith is the victory that addresses and conquers our fears. That's why Hebrews 11:29 says, "By faith the people crossed the Red Sea as on dry land, but the Egyptians, when they attempted to do the same, were drowned."

Are you at a Red Sea? Are you afraid? Do you sense an approaching doom? Let me encourage you to grab your Bible and find a quiet place. Pour out your heart to God and confess your fears to him. Ask him to calm your heart and to bring back to your mind all of the times when he has intervened for you. Slowly and prayerfully read through Hebrews 11. Then ask God to show you what he wants you to do and how he wants you to respond. He will lead you past your dread.

## THE ROADBLOCK OF RESTRICTING GOD TO A PATTERN

Hebrews 11:30 is a summary of the capture and fall of the city of Jericho: "By faith the walls of Jericho fell down after they had been encircled for seven days."

After Joshua and the Israelites crossed over the Jordan River into the land of Canaan, God told them to set their sights on the city of Jericho (Josh. 6:2). This would be their first military campaign. God outlined how they were to "attack" the city. To say that the strategy was unconventional would be an understatement. The walls of that great city eventually fell down, not because the Israelites used powerful battering rams, but because Joshua and his army did what God told them to do. And what was that? He instructed the entire army, along with the priests, to march around the city without making a sound for six days; then, on the seventh day, the priests were to blow the trumpets and the army was to shout (vv. 3–5). Then the walls of the city would collapse. Joshua and the people did as God instructed, and God did what he promised. The walls crumbled (v. 20).

Notice, Joshua didn't argue with God, nor did he offer to God an alternative strategy that he was more accustomed to. After forty years in the wilderness, Joshua had learned that God doesn't always work the way we want him to and he doesn't always do the same thing the same way. When it comes to how God does what he does, there is no "code" to be cracked. If there's one thing for sure, it is that we should not be so sure that God will do the same thing the same way the next time.

We like to be able to identify the "repetitive process" that will guarantee us a predictable outcome. In fact, some of us have a hard time trusting God unless he works the same way he did before. We want to foresee what God is going to do and how he is going to do it. This is a control issue. We want to be in "the know" and comfortable with God's approach to our faith challenge. We need to be careful. Faith means that we respond to God, and God maintains the prerogative to respond to our needs any way he chooses. God will not be confined or manipulated. So he keeps us off balance. God wants us to depend on him, not on a process or pattern.

Some years ago, a man said to me, "Crawford, you need to teach people how God works." In response, I said: "If you mean that I need to teach on God's character as revealed in his Word and the various ways in which he has intervened in the lives of his people during their journey, I completely agree. However, if you want me to come up with some standardized formula, I can't do that, and it would be arrogant for me to try."

Are we walking away from God's intervention in our lives because it doesn't make sense to us? Are we turning away from his deliverance, solutions, and provision because he's never done it this way before? We need to keep in mind that God does things out of the ordinary because he wants the glory. As in the case of the Israelites marching around the walls of Jericho, God's means may appear silly and foolish to us, but they shine a bright light on his glory. And that's all that matters.

## THE ROADBLOCK OF OUR BACKGROUND

Hebrews 11:31 presents a seventh and final roadblock to faith: "By faith Rahab the prostitute did not perish with those who were disobedient, because she had given a friendly welcome to the spies."

Hebrews 11 has been called "God's Hall of Faith." Think about it: a former prostitute is named among the great men and women of faith. What did she do? According to Joshua 2, she hid the Israelite spies who were checking out Jericho. The Bible says that what she did was an act of faith. Because of that act, her life was spared and she became a follower of the God of Abraham, Isaac, and Jacob.

Rahab is identified here as "the prostitute." This is not to highlight the immorality of her past, but to teach us that faith is the path to freedom and deliverance, no matter what we've done or where we've come from. Faith breaks the chains of bondage to sin and shame. Faith is the faucet from which flows Jesus's blood that washes away our guilt and condemnation (Rom. 8:1). Faith makes the difference.

But Rahab's inclusion in this list and in the genealogy of Jesus (Matt. 1:5) also says to us that our past, our background, should not limit our ability to trust God. Self-condemnation and false guilt have a way of revisiting us and pushing us back toward bondage. We crack open the door and allow the Devil to point his accusing finger at us. Before we know it, we buy the lies: "I'm not good enough for God to use. God would never make real what I dream about. Why even think about taking steps of faith in that direction?"

Yes, it's true that we are unworthy, but we are not worthless. Jesus died for us and redeemed us, and he has called us to find and live out the good works he has prepared for us (Eph. 2:10). Rahab teaches us that there is no limit to what God can do in and through us when, through the eyes of faith, we shift our gaze from where we came from and what we used to be to where God is taking us and what we can become. Our mission is clear: choose faith.

## QUESTIONS FOR DISCUSSION OR REFLECTION

1. Do you have a clear sense of your calling in life? If so, write it down or share it with your group.

2. Is there anything you know you are unwilling to sacrifice in order to experience God's best for you?

3. Gratitude is a great antidote for self-reliance. Take a moment to list the things God has done for you recently. If you are reading with others, share your list with the group.

4. Reflect on ways God has directed your path in the past. Has he always led you in the same way?

5. You may feel God cannot forgive the sins of your past. Read Romans 8:1. Claim this promise for your life. Ask God for confidence in your salvation.

# 7

# Faith Is Endurance

Let's step back for a second.

We've been tracing faith through Hebrews 11. Much of the chapter is about those who, in their lifetimes, experienced the fulfillment of what they were trusting God to do. Abraham and Sarah experienced the birth of Isaac. Moses was delivered from death. The children of Israel escaped the Egyptian army and certain death in the Red Sea. Because of faithful obedience to God, the walls of Jericho came tumbling down, and God spared the life of a former prostitute, Rahab. All ends well—that is, if you stop reading after the first part of verse 35.

But read carefully these words from Hebrews 11:35b–12:3:

Some were tortured, refusing to accept release, so that they might rise again to a better life. Others suffered mocking and flogging, and even chains and imprisonment. They were stoned, they were sawn in two, they were killed with the sword. They went about in skins of sheep and goats, destitute, afflicted, mistreated—of whom the world was not worthy—wandering about in deserts and mountains, and in dens and caves of the earth.

And all these, though commended through their faith, did not receive what was promised, since God had provided something better for us, that apart from us they should not be made perfect.

Therefore, since we are surrounded by so great a cloud of witnesses, let us also lay aside every weight, and sin which clings so closely, and let us run with endurance the race that is set before us, looking to Jesus, the founder and perfecter of our faith, who for the joy that was set before him endured the cross, despising the shame, and is seated at the right hand of the throne of God.

Consider him who endured from sinners such hostility against himself, so that you may not grow weary or faint-hearted.

Here we see clearly that faith does not mean the eradication of suffering and challenge. Some followers of Christ are called to a life of hardship. It appears as if all that these saints of old ever knew was adversity. But if you look closely, you discover that they were in a wonderfully special category. Their suffering attracted the presence and attention of God. And their endurance was a sacred gift, a treasure, given to us.

I met Dean Hertzler during our first semester in college. We came from very different backgrounds. I grew up in northern New Jersey, in the shadows of New York City. Dean grew up in the beautiful farm and Amish country of Lancaster County, Pennsylvania. We became close friends. I spent a lot of time with his dear family, and his dad took me on my first pheasant hunt. During spring breaks, Dean and I held evangelistic services at his home church in Lancaster County. I was honored when Dean and his fiancée, Janet, asked me to perform their wedding ceremony. These were joyous times, but Dean's life would be marked by challenge, adversity, and suffering.

Just before our college graduation ceremonies, Dean was

told that there had been a mix-up in the registrar's office, so his graduation would be delayed. After he finished the "surprise requirements," Dean got his degree and headed off to seminary. While he was there, he and Janet and their young family were hit with financial challenges, and once again his dreams had to be put on hold as they struggled to make ends meet. It took him several years longer than anticipated to finish school.

Finally it appeared as if they had turned the corner. Dean was called to be the pastor of a small church in New Jersey. Shortly after he accepted this call, he and Janet adopted David, a little African-American boy. But apparently this was too much for the church and its "leadership" to handle, so they asked Dean to leave. He and his family were filled with a sense of rejection and heartbreak. Then, not long after Dean had been dismissed from the church, little David was diagnosed with cancer. Within months, he died, bringing much more pain for Dean and his family.

Over the next few years, Dean had a number of ministry positions that all seemed to put him and Janet through varying degrees of disappointment and suffering. As a spectator to their trials and adversity, I found myself shaking my head and wondering, "How much more can they take?"

Dean and his family moved to Indiana, where he became a hospital chaplain. He flourished in this calling. He loved caring for and comforting those who were sick and hurting. When we talked, I heard joy and fulfillment in his voice. We were so happy for him.

Then he began to feel tingling and numbness in his hands. After seeing a doctor, he was given a series of tests. He was diagnosed with amyotrophic lateral sclerosis (ALS), or Lou Gehrig's disease. The disease progressed rapidly, rendering Dean totally immobile and confining him to a wheelchair. Dean knew that unless God intervened, he didn't have long on this earth. But he was anything but depressed. In our phone conversations, he talked about the sweetness of his fellowship with the Lord and how he was going to do all that he could do to serve the Lord. He surrendered to God's sovereign plan, whatever it might be. Tears trickled down my cheeks as I saw my friend latch on to enduring faith and suffer with holy dignity.

Soon, his muscles stopped working and he slipped into God's presence.

Months before he died, Dean had made a video of himself singing his favorite song. He asked Janet to be sure to show it at his memorial service. She did. Here are the words my friend sang:

PRECIOUS LORD, TAKE MY HAND
*Precious Lord, take my hand,*
*Lead me on, let me stand,*
*I'm tired, I'm weak, I'm worn.*
*Through the storm, through the night,*
*Lead me on to the light:*

*Take my hand, precious Lord,*
*Lead me home.*

*When my way grows drear,*
*Precious Lord, linger near;*
*When my life is almost gone,*
*Hear my cry, hear my call,*
*Hold my hand lest I fall:*

*Take my hand, precious Lord,*
*Lead me home.*

*When the darkness appears*
*And the night draws near,*

*And the day is past and gone.*
*At the river I stand,*
*Guide my feet, hold my hand:*

*Take my hand, precious Lord,*
*Lead me home.*

God did hold Dean's hand and led him home.

Like Dean, there are millions of followers of Christ whose lives are marked by suffering. The theme of their lives is enduring faith. They become trophies of God's sustaining grace and power. That's what Hebrews 11:35b–12:3 is all about.

## A SPECIAL CATEGORY

God places these heroes in a *special category*.

Keep in mind that Hebrews 11 is all about commending those who have exercised faith. It is no wonder it has been called "God's Hall of Faith." Every person or group of people mentioned in this great chapter receives God's applause for facing what faced them with faith. The miracle is that they weren't crushed by what they faced and experienced. Their faith sustained them and delivered them *in* their suffering and trials. They kept moving toward God even when God, in his infinite wisdom, did not remove what they faced. They wouldn't give up and they wouldn't give in. Like Job, they said, "Though he slay me, I will hope in him" (Job 13:15).

Persecution couldn't stop them. According to verses 35b–37a, they were tortured, mocked, flogged, placed in prison, stoned, sawn in two, and killed with the sword. Yet they would not recant. They remained faithful to the very end.

Destitution couldn't stop them. Verse 37b says, "They went

about in skins of sheep and goats, destitute, afflicted, mistreated." They were poor. They had nothing. Yet they were full of faith.

This is a very hard pill for some people to swallow. Destitution and faith—how can those two realities coexist? Doesn't God promise to take care of us and provide for us? And if we are walking with him, shouldn't we experience his best, including prosperity? After all, we are his children.

Unfortunately, throughout the history of the church, this kind of shallow, one-dimensional understanding of faith keeps resurfacing. Usually it is championed by those preachers who hop around the globe in their private planes, sporting the latest in reptile footwear and clad in their $2,000 custom-made suits. They stand before thousands in packed arenas and those watching on television, and declare that if we want to be blessed and "walk in the health and prosperity" that is our destiny, then we must "sow a seed" in their ministry. And the seeds are sown. In exchange, we get an "anointed prayer cloth," while they get the bumper crop. I guess jet fuel is expensive, and somebody has to pay for the condo in Palm Springs.

Yes, God does honor and reward the faith of his children by giving them everything they need to *face and go through* all he allows to come their way. God is focused on his glory, not on our lifestyle. And whatever brings him glory through our lives is what he will allow us to go through. If God is glorified by removing our suffering, he will do it. If he sees fit to be glorified by not delivering us, then he will do that. But if that is his will for us, he will be right there in the fire with us. We will experience a sweet intimacy with him, one that can be known only through suffering and deprivation. It is in the furnace of affliction that sustaining, enduring faith is born.

A faith that is understood only as a means to get what we

want from God has no room for suffering and adversity. Those who do suffer are considered less than what they could be. Somehow they must have given up their birthright, or perhaps they are not making the right "faith declarations" and "positive professions" to change their circumstances.

But here's a rock-solid certainty—*every true follower of Christ will suffer*. And they are not losers.

Again, Hebrews 11 is dominated by the accounts of those who were delivered from their challenges, but now the writer introduces us to the other side of the street. He now honors the countless "no-name" people who weren't delivered *from* their adversity, but were delivered *in* their adversity. He describes them as those "of whom the world was not worthy" (v. 38). It's as if God said to them: "You may have been hidden, marginalized, rejected, and scorned in this life, but I have walked with you each step of the way. I held your hand as you stood before the firing squad. I filled your heart and mind with my Word as ALS drained the life out of your body. I comforted you and strengthened you when you were imprisoned for your faith. I've trusted you with an uncommon life and journey. Through your suffering, I have given the world a portrait of my sustaining power and grace. You were faithful to me in the fire. The world is not worthy of you."

That line, "of whom the world was not worthy," encourages those who are suffering to turn from seeking the approval of the world to seeking the approval of God. We live to please him, and suffering stirs our appetite and longing for the presence of our loving, living God. We know that God alone will get us through, and we want to be faithful to the only One who really matters. This is what enduring faith does.

But there is another implication of the expression "of whom

the world was not worthy." These women and men are from another world. Heaven is their home and heaven will be their reward. In other words, their suffering reminds them that this world cannot give them what God has waiting for them when they are finally home. There may be no standing ovations in this life, but heaven is standing up because they are honoring God in the midst of hardship, heartache, and difficulty.

I think of Stephen, the first Christian martyr. Stephen preached a clear, direct message exalting Christ and pointing out the fact that the people had sinned by rejecting the Messiah (Acts 7). This didn't sit well. The angry mob picked up stones and began hurling them at Stephen. He was defenseless. But before he died, God gave him a vision of what was awaiting him. Let your soul be captured by these words: "But he, full of the Holy Spirit, gazed into heaven and saw the glory of God, and Jesus *standing* at the right hand of God. And he said, 'Behold, I see the heavens opened, and the Son of Man *standing* at the right hand of God.' . . . And falling to his knees he cried out with a loud voice, 'Lord, do not hold this sin against them.' And when he had said this, he fell asleep" (Acts 7:55–56, 60).

This is a remarkable account. According to Colossians 3:1 and Hebrews 8:1, Jesus is *seated* on his throne at the right hand of the Father. But when Stephen was being stoned for his faith-filled commitment to Christ and the gospel, he looked up into heaven and saw his Savior *standing* to personally welcome him to his reward.

This was true not only for Stephen. The Bible teaches that a hero's welcome awaits all who have been faithful (Matt. 25:21). As I mentioned earlier in this book, in recent years, our brand of Christianity has chosen to deemphasize, if not devalue, heaven and the eternal as a motivation for pressing forward through life's journey. We have conditioned people to assume that there must be some plan, strategy, or "practical steps" that will reduce if not eliminate our suffering and pain. That's why God has to remind us that this world is not the payoff. So he points us to faithful, God-honoring followers of Christ who suffered unimaginable heartache and pain in this life to whet our appetite for what awaits us—heaven's approval and the glory of his presence. The world is not worthy of these choice servants of the King because of their holy, noble hearts and because all that the world has to offer is insufficient to give them the honor and recognition that they deserve.

Perhaps you are being pounded by the waves of adversity and suffering. Let me encourage you. God sees and knows everything that you are going through. You may be feeling terribly alone, hidden and forgotten. Grab hold of the hope and comfort from Psalm 56:8: "You have kept count of my tossings; put my tears in your bottle. Are they not in your book?" Embrace the sweet words from Psalm 126:5: "Those who sow in tears shall reap with shouts of joy!" Trust our great God for grace for the moment and ask him to give you a glimpse of what awaits you.

## A SPECIAL MISSION

Not only has God placed these heroes in a special category, he also has given them a *special mission*.

Hebrews 11:39–40 says, "And all these, though commended through their faith, did not receive what was promised, since God had provided *something better for us, that apart from us they should not be made perfect.*"

Rebecca Nichols Alonzo, in her book *The Devil in Pew Number Seven*, writes the bone-chilling true story of the price her parents paid to fulfill their calling to serve others. Her father was the pastor of a small, rural church in Sellerstown, North Carolina. One very evil man in the church made it his life's mission to run her father out of the church and out of the community. The man went beyond the garden-variety harassment of vicious lies to literally setting off explosions around their house and even shooting through their windows. This went on for six years. Rebecca and her family lived under siege. They didn't know what each night would bring.

Yet Rebecca's parents prayed every day that this man would experience the love and forgiveness of Christ. They refused to be bitter, even while he tormented them and their family. They continued to forgive him and miraculously pressed into the Lord for the courage and strength to love and serve the people in their church and community.

Then the unthinkable happened. There was a young mother in their community whose husband was physically abusive. Rebecca's parents provided shelter for this woman and her baby. On the evening of March 23, 1978, while they all sat around the dinner table, the woman's husband walked through the door, pulled out a handgun, and shot Rebecca's father twice, then turned the gun on her mother and shot her once in the chest. Within minutes, her mother died. Miraculously, her father survived. Eight-year-old Rebecca and her three-year-old brother, Danny, saw it all.

When their dad was released from the hospital, they moved to Mobile, Alabama, where they could be close to family members and try to put their lives back together. But the years of relentless attacks and the tragic, violent death of his dear wife and ministry partner plunged Rebecca's father into a deep, inescapable darkness. Six years later, he died. Rebecca and Danny lost both of their parents and were left in the care of their father's sister.

This story seems senseless, heartbreaking, and unjust. Rebecca and Danny's parents were faithful, godly followers of Christ; they loved the Lord and loved the people they were called to serve. As you read their story, you realize they took every opportunity to share the Word of God and the hope of the gospel with those around them. They loved, prayed for, and—astonishingly—forgave those who persecuted them. But where was the fruit of their ministry? It appears they died without experiencing the rewards of their faithfulness. We're left shaking our heads and wondering why they went through so much effort, pain, and suffering with so few results?

But is that the correct way to think about this story?

As we have seen, faith and faithfulness never go unrewarded. Our problem is that we make the assumption that the significance of our lives and the impact of our work can be measured, experienced, and realized *during our lifetimes*. But if we look closely at Hebrews 11:39–40, we see that faith is a continuum. That means, as we have seen already, that the harvest may just be for another generation.

This is what happened in the case of Rebecca and her brother. The man who was responsible for putting their family through six years of torment finally was convicted and sent to prison. While he was behind bars, he repented of his sin and trusted Christ. Years later, after he was released, he contacted Rebecca, seeking her forgiveness for what he had done to her family. She told him that because of the model and influence of her parents, she and her brother had *already* forgiven him.

The book Rebecca wrote, chronicling this amazing story of gut-wrenching tragedy and uncommon, remarkable forgiveness, became a *New York Times* best seller. Many thousands have read the book and been transformed by the message of supernatural, unconditional love and forgiveness.

One of the producers of the *Dr. Phil* show read the book

and discovered that the man who had shot Rebecca's father and mother had been released from prison. This producer set in motion a chain of events that culminated in a program that focused on this amazing story of pain and forgiveness. Then the very man who had taken the life of Rebecca and Danny's mother walked out onto the set. More than thirty years later, they told him that they had forgiven him a long time ago. Millions watched that program, seeing and hearing about the supernatural power of the gospel to do what most of us would consider impossible—forgive the killer of one's mother.

Yes, the seeds that were sown faithfully in obscurity and in pain have now resulted in a harvest that cannot be measured. What appeared to be a fruitless or only marginally fruitful time has now blossomed and flourished for the glory of God. What God has done through Rebecca and Danny is a prime illustration of Hebrews 11:39–40. Through them, God completed what he initiated through their parents.

Sometimes God allows us to taste the fruit of our faith and obedience. But please don't assume, because you don't "see" the fruit of your obedience or you don't see visible results in someone else's life and ministry, that faith doesn't "work" or that the "strategy" and "approach" are wrong. Faith is always anchored to obedience and is not always measured in tangible results during our lifetimes. The miracle is that we don't give up or give in if we don't experience or "receive what was promised" (Heb. 11:39). Those who are given this uncommon calling inspire those who come after them to finish what God initiates in them. That's what the writer means when he says, "God had provided something better for us, that apart from us they should not be made perfect" (v. 40). Oh, the joy and privilege of taking the baton and running the anchor leg to the finish line.

## PREPARATION FOR ENDURING

So what do we do? In short, because we don't know what course our race will take, Hebrews 12:1–3 tells us to prepare ourselves to endure.

That means we should *shed the stuff*. Hebrews 12:1 says, "Therefore, since we are surrounded by so great a cloud of witnesses, let us also lay aside every weight, and sin which clings so closely, and let us run with endurance the race that is set before us."

Like sprinters, we need to get rid of anything that would impede our progress. That's what the word *weight* refers to. It could be good stuff that has now become unnecessary and a distraction to what God has called us to be and to do. It might be hobbies that take time away from focusing on what God wants us to do, memberships in groups or organizations that absorb the energy that should be invested in leveraging God's priorities for our lives, or a lack of personal discipline causing time and focus to seemingly evaporate. You can add to the list. Each of us has only one life, and God definitely has a plan for it. We have to keep the decks clear so that we can pour our lives and our faith into the race he has marked out for us.

But we also need to *get rid of sin*. Notice the line "and sin which clings so closely." Sin disqualifies us from the race. Nothing will inject embalming fluid into your life like sin. Sin stops the show. Hopes, dreams, and holy ambitions have all been killed and buried because of sin. Whenever God gives us an assignment, it is not only a faith journey, but also a call to cleansing and purity. God doesn't separate what he wants to do through us from what he wants to do in us. Unrepentant sin drains our spiritual energy, and we lose the capacity to finish the race. There is no holy handoff to the next generation.

But sometimes we get tired, weary, and discouraged during the race. What do we do? How do we continue?

We *focus on Jesus.*

Hebrews 11 is in the Bible to encourage us to keep moving in our faith journey. Each one of the brief biographies is meant to strengthen our resolve to believe and trust God. These are heavenly encouragements, motivating us to stay in the race. We need to tune our ears to listen to them.

But there is One who stands head and shoulders above them all. He is our model, our strength, and our Savior. We listen to faith's heroes, but we look to Jesus.

It is my prayer that if your faith has worn thin and you just don't feel as if you can keep moving, you will slip to your knees with your Bible open to Hebrews 12:2–3. Read this passage several times, slowly and prayerfully. Claim Jesus's strength and power. Allow your heart to be refreshed and encouraged by his obedience. He didn't quit, because we were worth it. And believe me, we shouldn't quit, because what God wants to do in and through us is more than worth it. "Consider him who endured from sinners such hostility against himself, so that you may not grow weary or fainthearted." Let's finish the race.

## QUESTIONS FOR DISCUSSION OR REFLECTION

1. Do you know anyone who has endured suffering in life with joy and confidence in God's grace?

2. Paul explains in Romans 8:17 that we will share in Christ's glory if we share in his suffering. Why do you think suffering comes before glory?

3. Do you feel that you are sowing in faithfulness without seeing fruit? Sometimes others see fruit before we do. Ask a friend for perspective.

4. Prayerfully read Hebrews 12:1–2. What "stuff" do you need to get rid of to run with endurance?

# 8

# Don't Panic

My wife, Karen, does not like clutter. She believes that if something has not been used or worn for a while, we should either give it away or throw it away. She definitely is not into hoarding. She's not careless about what she decides to get rid of, but when our kids were growing up, the joke around the house was that when Mom got into one of her cleaning moods, you'd better hide what you wanted to keep or else it would be gone.

When our son Bryan left to attend graduate school in California, he stored some of his stuff in our garage. The garage was getting a bit "cluttered" and needed to be cleaned out. So Karen called Bryan and discussed the stuff that he wanted to keep and what she could dispose of. But he forgot to tell her not to touch the shoe boxes.

From the time Bryan was a little boy, he had collected baseball cards. He had hundreds of them, some of which were worth a considerable amount of money. They were in shoe boxes stacked in the corner of the garage. You guessed it: to Karen, they looked like worthless cards that Bryan was no longer interested in, so she threw them out. Let's just say that when Bryan found out what she'd done, he wasn't a happy camper.

This all happened because assumptions had been made. It was an expensive lesson.

If we're not careful, we can throw away what is valuable. Hebrews 10:35–36 warns us: "Therefore do not *throw away your confidence*, which has a great reward. For you have need of endurance, so that when you have done the will of God you may receive what is promised."

What is confidence? Confidence is how faith expresses itself. It is the fruit of a faith that is anchored in an unfailing God and the trustworthiness of his promises. Confidence is a quiet boldness that is not intimidated or confused.

Look again at the phrase "do not throw away your confidence." This implies at least two things. First, we must guard, protect, and value our confidence. Keep it. Use it. It is a treasured gift. It will see us through. Second, this phrase also implies a shift in focus. In other words, we must not allow a challenge or opposition to overwhelm us and drain us of our confidence.

Fear and intimidation are some of Satan's most effective weapons. He uses them either to stop us dead in our tracks or to cause us to run from what God has for us (1 Pet. 5:8). Remember the old Western movies featuring cowboys out on the range, driving their cattle to market? The bad guys want the cattle, so they pull out their guns and shoot in the air. The cattle stampede away. Satan uses the circumstances and opposition in our lives to "shoot in the air," striking fear in our hearts and causing us to run away.

So how do we maintain our confidence when we are in the heat of the battle and we're confronted with stuff we've never seen or experienced before? I believe the answer to this question is found in the relationship between confidence and memory. Put another way, confidence has to do with the strength and vibrancy of our memory. For example, one of the reasons why baseball players go to spring training or football players go to training camp is so that they can sharpen their skills and focus under repetitive, simulated game situations. When the season starts and the games count, they say to themselves, "We *remember* what to do."

God gives all of us historic, dramatic experiences of his intervention and deliverance in order to foster in us the confident boldness to deal with where we are now and where we are going. But under pressure, it is easy to forget, isn't it?

One of my favorite movies is *Remember the Titans*. It's about a high school football team that, against the odds, wins a state championship. The halftime scene during the championship game is priceless. The team is behind, and it looks as if they are going to lose the game. The head coach (played by Denzel Washington) wants to let them down easy and preserve their dignity. In so many words, he tells his team that no matter what the score is, they are winners and they can hold their heads high. He's gently conceding defeat.

But this doesn't sit well with one of the team leaders. He steps forward and asks permission to speak. He looks at the coach and says, with the team listening: "You demanded perfection. Now, I ain't saying that I'm perfect, 'cause I'm not. None of us are. But we have won every single game we have played till now. So this team is perfect. We stepped out on that field that way tonight. And if it's all the same to you, Coach Boone, that's how we want to leave it." The players remembered what got them to the championship. Their confidence was resurrected. They won the game.

Perhaps you're in the thick of adversity. Maybe it's halftime and it looks like you are going to lose the "game." Let me suggest that you grab a pen and some paper, find a quiet place, and force your mind to go back to those sacred milestones in your life, those times when God showed up for you. Write them down. Look at what you've listed and embrace the reality that if he did it before, he can do it again. Nothing is too hard for our great God. Use memory to restore your confidence.

But let's take a step back and look at two very important, fundamental questions. First, does God's Word give us guidelines as to what we should remember to fuel and strengthen our confidence? Second, what happens in us when we live and operate according to these guidelines? God answers these questions in the book of Deuteronomy:

> The whole commandment that I command you today you shall be careful to do, that you may live and multiply, and go in and possess the land that the LORD swore to give to your fathers. And you shall remember the whole way the LORD your God has led you these forty years in the wilderness, that he might humble you, testing you to know what was in your heart, whether you would keep his commandments or not. And he humbled you and let you hunger and fed you with manna, which you did not know, nor did your fathers know, that he might make you know that man does not live by bread alone, but man lives by every word that comes from the mouth of the LORD. Your clothing did not wear out on you and your foot did not swell these forty years. Know then in your heart that, as a man disciplines his son, so the LORD your God disciplines you. . . .
>
> Take care lest you forget the LORD your God by not keeping his commandments and his rules and his statutes, which I command you today, lest, when you have eaten and are full and have built good houses and live in them, and when your herds and flocks multiply and your silver and gold is

multiplied and all that you have is multiplied, then your heart be lifted up, and you forget the LORD your God, who brought you out of the land of Egypt, out of the house of slavery, who led you through the great and terrifying wilderness, with its fiery serpents and scorpions and thirsty ground where there was no water, who brought you water out of the flinty rock, who fed you in the wilderness with manna that your fathers did not know, that he might humble you and test you, to do you good in the end. Beware lest you say in your heart, "My power and the might of my hand have gotten me this wealth." You shall remember the LORD your God, for it is he who gives you power to get wealth, that he may confirm his covenant that he swore to your fathers, as it is this day. And if you forget the LORD your God and go after other gods and serve them and worship them, I solemnly warn you today that you shall surely perish. Like the nations that the LORD makes to perish before you, so shall you perish, because you would not obey the voice of the LORD your God. (8:1–5, 11–20)

The Israelites had wandered in the wilderness for forty years. Finally they were on the brink of entering Canaan, the Promised Land. Moses gathered them together and delivered sobering instructions from God. Like a father giving instructions to his child heading off to college, God through Moses was warning his children to keep in the front of their minds what was really important. The message was that their deliverance and spiritual sustainability were in direct relationship to their willful determination to remember.

So this passage tells us what we need to remember and what happens in us when we remember. What God told the Israelites about remembering is universal spiritual food that will fuel our confidence.

## WHAT TO REMEMBER

When it comes to the depth and vibrancy of our confidence, there are four things we need to remember.

### *God's Leading*

First, we need to remember *how God has led us.*

The first part of Deuteronomy 8:2 says, "And you shall remember the whole way that the LORD your God has led you these forty years in the wilderness." God told his people to keep a record of his guiding hand. When they didn't know where they were going, God did, and he protected them and directed their steps. He led them by means of a pillar of cloud by day and a pillar of fire by night. When the pillar of cloud or fire moved, they were to move. When it stopped, they were to stop.

Perhaps not as dramatically, the same is true for us. When we look back over our lives, we realize that not knowing what to do next did not mean that we were without direction. Our great God was orchestrating the events and circumstances of our lives to get us where he wanted us to be. When we cried out to him for direction, he answered our prayers. When we were impatient and acted impulsively, and thus ended up getting into jams, in his mercy he came to us and put us back on track.

I think there is also a warning here. Moses was telling the people that God was no longer going to use a pillar of cloud or fire to lead them. They were now on the threshold of the Promised Land. But that didn't mean that they no longer needed God's direction. Seasons of success and prosperity have a way of driving us toward self-reliance. We set up shop and assume that we are doing just fine right where we are. We stop watching and listening for God's direction. Our relative stability makes us spiritually insensitive and vulnerable. Memory erodes. And because our confidence has been directed toward ourselves and not God, we fall apart when we are visited by dark, uncertain times. We forget what it was like to be led by the One who truly knows the way through the wilderness, God our Father.

During my early days of ministry, a dear friend and mentor, John Perkins, encouraged me to keep my guard up and be careful of the sense of entitlement that, ironically, can come with blessings. He said that I could get to the place where I no longer would be hungry for or dependent on God's direction and leading in my life. Then I'd have a real mess on my hands—me!

But maybe you are full of fear because you don't know what to do. Recently, I was visited by the dark clouds of uncertainty. I found myself wrestling with fear and apprehension concerning how I was going to meet a particular challenge. My faith and confidence were under attack and, frankly, I was running close to empty. I was out of answers and I needed God's direction. Then something happened that was a game-changer. Early one morning, I slipped out of bed, opened my journal, and began to write. Do you know what I wrote? I listed the milestones of God's direction and leading in my life. The Spirit of God freshened my memory, and in so doing, he replenished my confidence.

### God's Testing

Second, we need to remember *how God has tested us*.

At first glance, this sounds a bit odd, doesn't it? What is the relationship between God's "tests" in my life and my confidence? Isn't my confidence lodged in his faithfulness, not mine? Yes, and that's the point.

Look at the second part of verse 2: "that he might *humble* you, *testing* you to know what was in your heart, whether you would keep his commandments or not."

Let's face it: the Israelites did not have a consistent track record of obedience and faithfulness to the Lord during their forty years in the wilderness. They raised complaining to an art form. There were power struggles and downright rebellions. They didn't like the menu God served them. They didn't care for the leaders God gave them. They didn't like the route to which God assigned them. They were often paralyzed by fear. God even gave Moses an opportunity for a "do-over": "And the LORD said to Moses, 'I have seen this people, and behold, it is a stiff-necked people. Now therefore let me alone, that my wrath may burn hot against them and I may consume them, in order that I may make a great nation of you'" (Ex. 32:9–10). Moses interceded on behalf of the people and God did not wipe them out.

So here in Deuteronomy 8:2, just before they were to march into the Promised Land, God reminded his people that they didn't have a good record when it came to passing tests. But, you ask, how did that build their confidence? Look at the phrase "that he might *humble* you." The message was that failure should have taught them that they were inadequate and that they didn't have what it took to consistently obey God and do his will.

Failure that is the result of self-reliance and inadequacy is a wonderful gift from God. I heard it put well by Dr. Bill Bright, the late founder of Cru, who often said, "Humiliation will make you humble."

Humble people are dependent people. God's tests in the wilderness were meant to send a message to the Israelites: "Don't trust yourself and don't depend on yourself." God wanted his people to see the glaring contrast between their inadequacy and inconsistency and his supreme sufficiency and unfailing faithfulness. He allowed them to fail not so that they would give up, but so that they would turn from themselves to him. He wanted them to redirect their confidence, placing it in a God who cannot lie, cannot fail, and is never without options or resources. They needed to know that God was everything that they were not, and the tests in the wilderness were trophies to this reality.

Every once in a while, it's good to remember the tests that we failed, and what those failures revealed about us and what they taught us concerning our need to depend on God. In this regard, our humiliation becomes our help. Walk over to that trophy case and revisit the times you failed God or took him for granted. Consider how merciful he has been to you. Remember how he poured out grace and strength, and came rushing to your side when you acknowledged that you were wrong and in over your head. Instead of saying, "Good, you're getting what you deserve," he said, "Stand back and see the salvation of the Lord."

God tests us to teach us that he doesn't need our competence and strength. He wants our weakness and dependence. It is only when we are dependent that we are most open to be filled with God confidence. Please don't forget the tests.

### God's Provision

Third, we need to remember *how God has provided for us.*

Before the Israelites set foot in the land that was the fulfillment of God's promise, God called them to take a bit of a time-out to think about and savor his care and provision for them. Once again, he wanted them to remember something. God did not want them to ever question whether he loved and cared for them. He reminded them that he had taken care of them every step of the way.

Feel the compassion in these words: "He humbled you and let you hunger and fed you with manna, which you did not know, nor did your fathers know, that he might make you know that man does not live by bread alone, but man lives by every word that comes from the mouth of the LORD. Your clothing did not wear out on you and your foot did not swell these forty years" (Deut. 8:3–4).

In the latter years of my father's life, he often talked about the joy and privilege it was to be able to provide for his family. Sometimes Karen and I would overhear him telling his grandchildren how important it is to provide for one's family and how grateful he was that he had been able to do this. When we were growing up, my sisters and I knew that Pop would do whatever he had to do in order to keep a roof over our heads, clothes on our backs, and food in our stomachs. He believed that a man takes care of what belongs to him.

God takes care of what belongs to him. He reminded his people of this so that they would not transfer their confidence in him to what this new land would provide for them. In other words, he wanted them to be aware that whether in the wilderness or in a place where there was plenty and prosperity, *God was the provider*. And the way to keep this reality fresh in their minds was to remember the timely supernatural provision of their loving Father during their tentative, transient existence in the wilderness.

So he reminded them that when they woke up every morning, they had had enough to eat to sustain them for that day. What about their clothes? God had not dropped cloth from the sky so that they could make new clothes. Neither had he sent merchants their way with some sort of mobile clothing store. He miraculously had kept fresh and strong the clothes and sandals they had brought with them when they left Egypt forty years before!

This is a very important lesson. Don't dictate to God how and what he should provide; just trust him to provide. His provision may not always be what we want, but it will always be what we need. The focus is gratitude to and for the faithful provider, not whether he gives us everything on our wish lists.

Has God taken care of you? Has he met your needs? Once again, keep a record of what he has done so that when it's time for another season in the wilderness, you won't throw away your God confidence, or when you walk into prosperity, you will not become entitled and self-reliant, and, in so doing, throw away your confidence.

## God's Discipline

Fourth, we need to remember *how God has disciplined us.*

God's "no" responses, deprivations, and corrections are gifts. They provide focus and direction, for they are reminders that some things are right and some things are wrong. There's a price to be paid when we head off in the wrong direction. It's called consequences. Those who remember the consequences and embrace the lessons are those who are growing in their faithfulness and their God confidence.

That's the point of verse 5: "Know then in your heart that, as a man disciplines his son, the Lord your God disciplines you."

As parents, we are responsible to align the behavior of our children with that which is right. We want their character, choices, and behavior to reflect godly integrity and enduring values. The vision is for them to be stable, secure difference makers when they become adults. So when they veer off track, we have to remind them of the destination. If they are not responsive, then we have to give them the gift of consequences. Why? Because we want them to associate wrong directions and wrong choices with pain. Without this sense of focused discipline, they will become unstable, having never developed the ability to say no to their impulses and yes to what is right and best. Without discipline, they will not become God-confident contributors to the world they are called to impact and reach.

As God prepared the Israelites to step into the Promised Land, he told them to remember the consequences, some excruciatingly painful, they had had to face for their disobedient, willful behavior. God was warning them that even though their nomadic journey was over, they must not forget the lessons from his discipline. If they did, they would have no sense of mission or direction. To forget is to wander, lost and aimless.

I know a man who is very gifted but very undisciplined. He has more dreams and ideas than you can imagine. But he has trouble staying focused and concentrating on anything long enough to see it through. His priorities are out of order, and his marriage and family are needlessly suffering. What's worse is that he seems to ignore the signs and growing consequences of his erratic, undisciplined choices. He seems lost and confused, and he told me recently that he doesn't know what God wants him to do. I suggested that he take a close look at the pain and consequences he is suffering, and identify the boundaries that he has crossed. God's direction may be clearer than he thinks, but maybe not what he wants to hear.

Believe it or not, nothing destroys your confidence more than ignoring the wisdom that is available from God's discipline in your life. To ignore the lessons and the message in the consequences is to choose our way over God's. Welcome to self-deception, the featured course on the menu of fools and the path to confusion and purposelessness.

Like the Israelites, we need to keep God's discipline in our lives fresh in our minds. It is good to share with others about the times when we disregarded God's leading and chose to go our own way. I could cite the time I ignored the wise, godly counsel of dear friends and almost got caught up in something that could have destroyed my ministry. God in his mercy plucked me out of that situation, but he let me dangle long enough to learn that there are times when listening is better than experience.

Remembering our failures and God's loving correction ties our hearts to him and creates in us a desire to be faithful to him.

## WHY WE REMEMBER

This points us toward the second question: What happens in us when we remember? In other words, why do we need to remember how God has led us, tested us, provided for us, and disciplined us?

The short answer is, because of what remembering develops and produces *in us.* Deuteronomy 8:11–20 outlines the three rock-solid characteristics of God-confident followers.

### *Our Obedience*

First, by remembering, we will experience a growing *unconditional obedience.* God says in verse 11, "Take care lest you forget the LORD your God by not keeping his commandments and his rules and his statutes, which I command you today."

God's Word and his work in our lives are to produce hearts that are obedient to him in all things. Disobedience is always sin and is never accommodated by God. There's a "cute" line that has been floating around for years, but it is actually sad and dangerous. You've heard it: "It's easier to ask for forgiveness than to ask for permission." The premeditated decision to disregard what we know to be right or to trespass others' prerogatives makes our "seeking forgiveness" a sham and a disingenuous game.

We need to be careful that we do not abuse God's gracious lovingkindness by redefining it and rebranding it as some sort of permission. God's faithfulness and grace should stir in us gratitude and a passion to pursue holiness and obedience (Titus 2:11–14). This is what God wanted his people to both remember and reflect when they walked into the Promised Land.

Our obedience is worship (Rom. 12:1–2). It declares that God alone is our confidence and victory. His grace has taught us to obey him.

### Our Loyalty

Second, we will experience an increasingly *undivided loyalty*.

In essence, God says: "I proved my love and care for you in the wilderness so that you would know in your heart that I alone am God, and that nothing or no one else deserves your heart and your worship. Don't forget." Memory moves us toward undivided loyalty.

Take a look at Deuteronomy 8:12–14: ". . . lest, when you have eaten and are full and have built good houses and live in them, and when your herds and flocks multiply and your silver and gold is multiplied and all that you have is multiplied, then your heart be lifted up, *and you forget the LORD your God*."

What's the message? Don't commit idolatry. There was a danger that the Israelites could come to think of God's provision as the source. Without rehearsing the goodness of God during their wilderness journey, once they were removed from the daily reminders of their neediness and dependence on God, they would helplessly drift toward conflicting loyalties or outright abandonment of God.

Loyalty is intentional. It is choosing to remember and cel-ebrate the love and sacrifices of others on your behalf. Loyalty doesn't forget who took care of you and brought you to where you are today. You are not conflicted, but are loyal only to God.

Some of us downplay God's role in the success and stuff we have accumulated. We may acknowledge him, but truthfully we want people to know how smart, competent, and resourceful we are. In doing this, we become "God" and God becomes "god." But God doesn't settle for double-billing. He is the show, or he doesn't show up at all. God has led us, tested us, provided for us, and disciplined us so that we would get the message that he wants all of the glory all of the time, whether we are wandering in the wilderness or living in a mansion in a gated community. We need to live and act in a way that declares that he is God and no one else or nothing else is.

### Our Dependence

Third, we will experience an increasingly *uncompromising de-pendence.*

Deuteronomy 8:17–18 says: "Beware lest you say in your heart, 'My power and the might of my hand have gotten me this wealth.' You shall remember the LORD your God, for it is he who gives you power to get wealth, that he may confirm his covenant that he swore to your fathers, as it is this day."

The Israelites were forced to depend on God in the wilder-ness. When their wandering ended, God told them, "Depend on me in the Promised Land." They lived from God's hand to their mouths so that dependence would be ingrained in them. Depen-dence on God was meant to become more than something that they pulled out and used when they were in a jam. Dependence was meant to become a part of their character, their identity.

Although their living conditions would drastically improve, dependence would remain a constant. Once again, God led them, tested them, provided for them, and disciplined them to make them a dependent people.

The endgame? A resilient faith that evidences itself in God confidence. Take an inventory of your life and chart the ways in which God has developed you and taken care of you. Please, don't forget these things. Talk about them. Share them. Treasure them. And don't lose track of them and inadvertently throw them away.

## QUESTIONS FOR DISCUSSION OR REFLECTION

1. Take a moment to jot down some "sacred milestones" in your life.

2. Recall a time God led you, clearly and faithfully. How did he do it? What were the circumstances?

3. What needs has the Lord met in your life? How is he providing for you right now?

4. It is easy to take credit for the good things in our lives. Read Deuteronomy 8:17–18. Now take a moment to pray, thanking God for his provision.

# 9

# Christ Our Courage

Sometimes we focus so much on the particulars and details of the Christian life that we lose sight of a fundamental, life-changing reality: *our faith journey is the expression of the life of Christ through us.*

Just before Jesus was crucified, he gathered his disciples together and gave them specific instructions and words of encouragement, preparing them for life and ministry after his death and resurrection. These focused words are found in John 13–16. In 15:1–11, Jesus told his followers that he was the life-giving focal point of their existence and fruitfulness. Any hope of surviving or thriving would depend on their intentional decision to "abide in the vine" (Christ). He wanted this to be unmistakably clear: there is no sustainable life and power apart from him. That's why he said: "I am the vine; you are the branches. Whoever abides in me and I in him, he it is that bears much fruit, *for apart from me you can do nothing*" (John 15:5). Jesus is the Christian life and should be everything to us.

Faith is the expression of our utter dependence on our living, all-powerful Savior. He never fails. Put another way, our faith is a living, victorious faith because it is lodged in the second person of the Godhead, the living, victorious Christ. It is not the strength of our faith that saves the day, but the power of our Savior. The journey may be uncertain and unpredictable, but our Savior is the same yesterday, today, and forever (Heb. 13:8). He's in control and is never surprised. We lean into his powerful arms and rest in him.

A friend told me recently that he was moved to tears while teaching his three-year-old son how to float. As they got into the water, he placed his hands under the back of his little boy and told him repeatedly to lean back, relax, and trust Daddy. As he did what his dad said, the boy kept saying, "I trust you, Daddy, I trust you, Daddy, I trust you, Daddy . . ." Even *after* his dad's hands were no longer holding him up, the boy kept saying, "I trust you, Daddy."

We always rest on, depend on, turn to, and trust Christ. Until we settle this in our hearts and minds, the Christian life in general and faith in particular will always be a struggle, and we will sink.

Once again, our Savior, the Lord Jesus Christ, is the focal point of the Christian life and of our faith. As we have seen, he is our passion and our ultimate motivation for moving forward in faith (Heb. 12:1–3). But we don't use Jesus to get what we want. We surrender to him so that we experience all that he has in store for us and all that he wants to do through us. We follow him, and as we do, he allows us to face gaps, inadequacy, and insufficiency. This is so that we might know and experience that he is the gap filler, our adequacy, and our sufficiency.

You see, there is a relationship between the depth of our surrender to Christ and the richness and vibrancy of our faith. Our devotion to Jesus must be total and complete. Now, what I just said might disturb you. You might be saying: "Hold the phone,

Crawford. There's no such thing as complete devotion to Christ in this life." Yes, that is true, in the sense that as we walk in the light, the Holy Spirit shows us more areas to be surrendered to the Lord. But the heart commitment, the response to Christ and his Word, must be settled. We are passionate pursuers of Jesus. We have decided to live and move in one direction, toward Jesus. We stop making excuses for our disobedience and view repentance as a gift from God to keep us pursuing the heart of our Savior and his will for our lives. We want to be all in.

Too many of us are like those fruit drinks that only contain 10 percent juice. We want to be flavored by Jesus, but not filled with Jesus. Is it any wonder that we struggle with faith? Is it any wonder that a watching world is often baffled and confused about what it means to be a Christ follower?

Essentially, this is the message that Jesus delivered to the church at Laodicea in Revelation 3:15–16: "I know your works: you are neither cold nor hot. Would that you were either cold or hot! So, because you are lukewarm, and neither hot nor cold, I will spit you out of my mouth."

Why such strong words? Simply put, Jesus is not playing games. He did not come and die for us so that we might "incrementalize" our relationship with him. He has a plan and a purpose for our lives. To say that we are related to him is to be committed to following him and to gladly and freely give ourselves to him, allowing him to do in and through us whatever he chooses to do.

## THE LIKENESS OF JESUS

That choice, that commitment, unleashes a faith that changes our lives and impacts those who come in contact with us. Why? Because as we follow Jesus, we grow into his likeness. We begin to look and act like our Savior. Romans 8:29 tells us that we have been marked "to be conformed to the image of [God's] Son." Jesus is living his life through us. Think about that. That's an astonishing reality. God wants our lives to be the biography of his Son.

A few years ago, a woman said something to me that no one had said to me before and no one has said since. She sat next to me on a flight from Atlanta to Cincinnati. I noticed that her eyes were puffy and red. She'd been crying. I asked whether she was OK. She said she wasn't, then proceeded to share with me that her life was falling apart. She was scared because she had made some bad choices and it looked as if her marriage was over. She felt she had no future. After listening, I shared with her the hope of the gospel and some promises from the Word of God. I could sense and see a little glimmer of hope within her.

When the plane landed, we said goodbye. But as I turned to walk toward baggage claim, she asked me a question that frankly startled me. She said, "Crawford, are you Jesus?" I was so caught off guard that it took me a moment to respond. I finally replied, "No, I'm not Jesus, but I know him and I need him just as much as everyone else does."

When I walked away, I was sobered by an inescapable sense of accountability and responsibility. I have to continue to work on getting Crawford out of the way so that the life of Christ can be experienced, seen, and demonstrated through me. No, I can't do this in my own power and strength. This kind of growing Christlike reality only happens by faith; it is us saying, "I trust you, Daddy." I believe that's what the apostle Paul was referring to when he said in Colossians 2:6, "Therefore, as you received Christ Jesus the Lord, so walk in him." We received Christ by faith. We pursue Christ by faith. We experience Christ by faith.

Then the power and person of Christ are released in and through us—by faith.

This is urgent business. As we have seen throughout this book, faith is not passive, but is intentional and decisive. That means that if we are going to *experience* Christ as the focal point and source of our lives, we must *decide* that this is what he is. Remember, Jesus *commanded* his followers to abide in him (John 15:4). Abiding is determined by choice, by decision.

## FOUR DECISIONS

With this in mind, I want to look at four Christ-exalting decisions that every one of his followers must make. These decisions are outlined by Paul in the book of Philippians.

### Start with Christ

The first decision is to *start with Christ*.

Philippians 1:6 says, "And I am sure of this, that he who began a good work in you will bring it to completion at the day of Jesus Christ."

Let me state the obvious: the decision here is implied. In other words, we already have made the foundational, fundamental decision to trust Christ as our Savior and Lord. When we placed our faith in him, we were forgiven of all of our sins, past, present, and future. We were given the gift of eternal life. We are forever his. That decision has changed everything.

This verse assures us that our relationship with Christ is not fragile and it certainly doesn't depend on us. We were dead in our sins and absolutely incapable of saving ourselves (Eph. 2:1–10). God, through Christ, came to us and even gave us the faith to trust that what Jesus did on our behalf was sufficient to establish a relationship with him. Salvation is all of God.

The point of this verse is that whatever God starts, he finishes. He wants us to live the Christian life with the confident assurance that the God of the ages will carry us safely home. He will not abandon us. In essence, our loving heavenly Father says: "Because you placed your faith in my Son, I will show you that there is no failure in me. I am absolutely, infinitely trustworthy. Rest in me and the provision of my Son. Your salvation is complete." God has no unfinished projects. He has no starts and stops. He is a covenant-keeping God. Those he saves, he saves completely and forever!

This should cause us to move forward in our walk with Christ with certainty and confidence. We can boldly face what confronts us because our future is secure. Not only will we be in his presence one day, but his presence is with us now. He is currently working in us, on us, and through us.

### Surrender Our Well-Being to Christ

This introduces the second decision: to *surrender our well-being to Christ.*

Paul wrote to the Philippians from prison in Rome. His friends in Philippi were concerned about him and wanted to know how he was doing. They were aware that their dear friend and brother might very well be headed toward execution. I suppose they couldn't help but wonder if Paul was discouraged, weighed down by thoughts of death and loss.

But this was not at all the case. When they opened the letter from Paul, they were hit with words of heartfelt gratitude and supernatural joy. Far from being a solemn obituary or funeral dirge, his letter is a Christ-exalting, joy-filled celebration of life. In fact, he wanted the Philippian believers to know and experience the joy that he was experiencing.

In the letter, Paul welcomes and greets his circumstances as an opportunity to bring glory to his Savior and to spread the gospel. His focus is not on what is happening to him, but on what God is doing through him. Look at what he says in Philippians 1:12–14: "I want you to know, brothers, that what has happened to me has really served to advance the gospel, so that it has become known throughout the whole imperial guard and to all the rest that my imprisonment is for Christ. And most of the brothers, having become confident in the Lord by my imprisonment, are much more bold to speak the word without fear."

These are not the words of a depressed, despondent man who has given up and is biding his time while awaiting the inevitable. No, this is the testimony of a follower of Christ whose faith is not theoretical or just-out-of-reach inspirational jargon. His is a decisive, resilient faith that is not caving in to what is happening to him. Paul's faith is keeping him focused and pointing him toward the God-given opportunities before him *because* of his imprisonment.

But the key word is *decisive*.

Paul responded the way he did because Jesus Christ was everything to him. He decided to view his circumstances through the eyes of faith, placing Jesus in the middle of his suffering and adversity. His determination to press forward in faith caused him to redeem the time and bring the transforming hope of Christ into what could have been the darkest, most trying time of his life.

Please note this response was not passive but intentional. Paul made a focused faith decision that he was determined to keep. Feel the intensity of these words: "It is my eager expectation and hope that I will not be at all ashamed, but that with full courage now as always Christ will be honored in my body, whether by life or by death. For to me to live is Christ, and to die is gain" (vv. 20–21).

No matter what he faced, he was going to honor Christ. He knew that his life was to be the autobiography of his dear Savior, and he was determined for it to be so. His life would be the expression of Christ, and in death he would gain Christ, finally home.

Have you made this decision, this determination, that no matter what happens to you, you will honor and glorify Christ? This decision can make faith expensive. Bitter, hard experiences and circumstances can push us toward anger and even resentment toward God. That's when our "faith determination" has to speak to our emotions and our circumstances, reminding us that the lordship of Christ is real and that submission, though painful, honors him. If we don't do this, we miss the joy and richness of his presence and the blessing of his redemptive work in us and through us.

There is a man in our church who has had more than sixty surgeries. He's undergone several transplants and has been at death's door more times than I can remember. Most of the past thirty years, Jim has been in and out of hospitals. But when you meet Jim and talk to him, you neither see nor hear hopelessness or despair. You come in contact with a man who loves Jesus with every fiber of his being. I love being around him and praying with him. He talks about the Lord, and his heart is filled with gratitude to God for how he cares for him and his dear family. Jim draws his strength and hope from Jesus. He, too, has made the focused faith decision that "for to me to live is Christ, and to die is gain."

Joy is not the absence of adversity, but delight in our Savior, even in our suffering. But this is a decision, a choice. Like Paul and Jim, we too must decide to surrender our well-being to Christ.

### Serve like Christ
Third, we must decide to *serve like Christ*.

To be a follower of Christ means that we live in community

with others. When we trusted Christ as Savior and Lord, we were placed into the family of God, the church. There is no such thing as a disconnected Christian. In other words, to say that we are followers of Christ but that we are not a part of the church means that we are not followers of Christ. Our salvation means that we have been reconciled with God and with others who have trusted Christ. We are called to live out that reconciliation in real time, in community with other Christ followers—imperfect people with real challenges and problems. In so doing, we celebrate and demonstrate the transforming power of Christ and his presence among his people. That's called the church.

The church is meant to be God's visible display of the hope and integrity of the gospel. So God wants his people not only to get along, but to love and relate to one another in the same way that Jesus loves and relates to us. As you well know, this is often very difficult—but so was crucifixion. Jesus shines brightest through us when things are the most difficult for us. This is particularly true when we have been hurt and offended by our fellow Christians.

Responding in the right, Christlike way to those who don't like us or to those who have hurt us or offended us is an expensive faith decision. But we are called to love and serve one another because that's what Jesus did for us. We are his family, his body, so that's what we do, too.

Paul was concerned that this others-oriented, Christlike serving spirit was lacking at the church in Philippi. Perhaps he was worried that the Philippians were drifting toward isolation and an unhealthy, self-serving Christianity that tolerated and used people rather than fighting to model and emulate the example of Christ. So he reminded them to determine to love and serve one another the same way Jesus loved and served them.

Paul pleads with them to make sure that their relationships with one another tell the truth about their relationship with Christ: "So if there is any encouragement in Christ, any comfort from love, any participation in the Spirit, any affection and sympathy, complete my joy by being of the same mind, having the same love, being in full accord and of one mind. Do nothing from selfish ambition or conceit, but in humility count others more significant than yourselves. Let each of you look not only to his own interests, but also to the interests of others. *Have this mind among yourselves, which is yours in Christ Jesus . . .*" (2:1–5).

Paul goes on, in verses 6–8, to describe the severe humility and the ultimate price that Jesus paid (death by crucifixion) to secure our salvation. His love for us drove him to give his life so that we would be made right with God. The question is, what are we willing to do to be made right with one another?

Most of the problems in churches can be traced to the inability of believers to do what is right in relationships. We have a tendency to justify and sanitize selfishness and various other forms of sinful behavior. We may be right on an issue, but our hearts and attitudes may be wrong. When we gloss over or minimize our part in fractured relationships and hurt feelings, community disintegrates.

We are most like Christ when we choose to forgive and relate to one another from hearts of love. We pursue unity and do not create or accommodate division. We don't ignore issues and conflicts in our relationships; rather, we do all that we can to resolve them and live in reconciled, restored relationships. Why? Because we are commanded to love and serve one another, and we are stewards of the integrity of the gospel and the reputation of Christ before a watching world. What does it say about the power of the gospel when we can't or won't get along with one another?

Yes, this is very difficult to do. As the old line says, the Christian life would be easy if it weren't for people. But when by faith we take our relationship struggles to Christ, he enables us to see others through his eyes and respond to them based on the grace we, too, have received. Others see us as representatives of Christ and not as demanding, entitled people fighting for position and recognition. They see Christ as our motivation and passion.

### Be Satisfied with Christ

Fourth, we must decide to *be satisfied with Christ*.

Jesus must become our supreme desire. We look to him and him alone to satisfy our longings. Just as we trust Christ alone for our salvation, we trust Christ alone to sustain us and satisfy us. Jesus will not compete with divided affections and loyalties. Remember, he commanded his disciples to abide in him.

When we turn to other things or relationships to fulfill the deepest longing of our souls, we end up frustrated, like a parched and thirsty man who can find only a few sips of water. Jesus is the fountain, the water of life. When he told the Samaritan woman, "Whoever drinks of the water that I will give him will never be thirsty again" (John 4:14), Jesus declared that he was the One she was born for and that he alone is the source of satisfaction.

In recent years, I have become increasingly concerned about what I call a "minimalist" approach to preaching and presenting the person of Christ. In our desire for people to like Jesus, we have emphasized his love—and he does love us—and his humanity. We have presented a Jesus who identifies with our pain and struggles, and who walks with us. Again, he does. But let's be careful. We're not called to be Jesus's PR firm or to polish his résumé. We need to make sure that we tell the whole truth about who our Savior is.

Jesus not only identifies with our pain and struggles, but, as the almighty God, he is adequate and sufficient to meet every need we have, plus more. This is the Jesus to whom we turn and in whom we place our full faith and confidence. If we do not see him in this light, he will never be the source of our lives and the satisfier of our souls. We must preach his adequacy and sufficiency to ourselves and to others. When we declare that Jesus is Lord, we are saying that all that God is is with us in the person of his Son, and God wants to fill our hearts with satisfaction and a holy passion for Jesus. We gladly release and give up all things for our Savior. Again, he is both our satisfaction and our pursuit.

In Philippians 3:4–11, Paul presents Christ as his satisfaction and pursuit. He begins by outlining his impressive background and accomplishments. He had every reason to be self-sufficient, taking great pride and pleasure in the fact that very few people had achieved what he had. He had power, prominence, and prestige. Then he met Jesus. Everything changed.

Look at what he says in verses 7–8: "But whatever gain I had, I counted as loss for the sake of Christ. Indeed, I count everything as loss because of the surpassing worth of knowing Christ Jesus my Lord. For his sake I have suffered the loss of all things and count them as rubbish, in order that I may gain Christ." This should be the all-consuming passion of our lives, too.

Keep in mind that Paul wrote these words while he was in prison. His condition or circumstances did not erode his passion to pursue Christ and to turn to him as his satisfaction and sufficiency. Jesus was the object of his faith and the strength and source of his life.

This is the reason why Paul could experience contentment while in the midst of uncertain circumstances. He had made the faith decision to keep his focus and heart centered on Jesus. The ability to be content and the strength to keep pursuing Jesus did not come from him. It came from Jesus.

This is his point in 4:11–13. In verse 11, he acknowledges that contentment isn't natural for him: "I have *learned* in whatever situation I am to be content." The key word is *learned*. He had seasons when he had plenty and times when he had next to nothing. He had to learn that his spiritual well-being and peace could not fluctuate with his changing circumstances. Worry and anxiety would win, and his faith would wither and die.

But the real lesson that he learned is summarized in verse 13: "I can do all things through [Christ] who strengthens me." The source of Paul's strength was not a growing self-confidence that was the product of a consistent run of "success" and favorable circumstances. He learned that in the scheme of things, it was relatively unimportant where he found himself. The difference maker was *who* was with him and to *whom* he looked. Jesus was with him. Jesus would strengthen him. Jesus would see him safely home.

And Jesus will do the same for us.

The faith questions always boil down to these: Who is with us? Who are we looking to?

Don't underestimate Jesus.

## QUESTIONS FOR DISCUSSION OR REFLECTION

1. Are you confident that you have surrendered your life to Christ? If so, thank him for his sacrifice. If not, take a moment to ask Jesus to be Lord of your life.

2. The author writes, "We want to be flavored by Jesus, but not filled with Jesus." In what ways do you want to enjoy the benefits of Jesus without giving your life to him completely?

3. Trusting Christ means serving. Take the next step of faith and join Christ in his mission through the local church. Ask a friend or a pastor where you might serve best.

4. After reading this book, how would you *define* faith? How would you *describe* Christian faith to a curious friend? Pray for an opportunity to share your faith with someone this week.

# Notes

1. Mark Twain, *Mark Twain Day by Day*, vol. II (Banks, OR: Horizon Micro Publishing, 2009), 230.
2. Genesis 15–17 gives us more details about what Abraham was facing.
3. Paul E. Miller, *A Praying Life: Connecting with God in a Distracting World* (Colorado Springs: NavPress, 2009), 80.
4. A. W. Tozer, *A Disruptive Faith: Expect God to Interrupt Your Life*, ed. James L. Snyder (Bloomington, MN: Bethany House, 2011), 23.
5. Quoted in Warren W. Wiersbe, *Be Confident: Live by Faith, Not by Sight* (Colorado Springs: David C. Cook, 2009), 147.
6. Martin Luther King Jr., "I've Been to the Mountaintop," speech in Memphis, TN, April 3, 1968, http://mlk-kpp01.stanford.edu/index .php/encyclopedia/documentsentry/ive_been_to_the_mountaintop/, accessed February 11, 2015.
7. C. S. Lewis, *Mere Christianity* (1952; repr., New York: Macmillan, 1979), 120.
8. Cited in Randy Alcorn, *Money, Possessions, and Eternity*, revised and updated edition (Wheaton, IL: Tyndale House, 2011), 159.

# General Index

# Scripture Index